The Last Lullaby

Poetry *from* *the* Holocaust

Edited and Translated by
Aaron Kramer

Drawings by
Saul Lishinsky

A Dora Teitelboim Foundation Publication

Syracuse University Press

First Paperback Edition 1999
99 00 01 02 03 04   6 5 4 3 2 1

This book is published with the assistance of a grant
from the Dora Teitelboim Foundation.

The paper used in this publication meets the minimum requirements
of American National Standard for Information Sciences—Permanence
of Paper for Printed Library Materials, ANSI Z39.48-1984. ∞™

Library of Congress Cataloging-in-Publication Data

The last lullaby : poetry from the Holocaust / edited and translated
by Aaron Kramer ; drawings by Saul Lishinsky.
p. cm.
ISBN 0-8156-0478-5 (cloth : alk. paper) 0-8156-0579-X (pbk : alk. paper)
1. Yiddish poetry—Translations into English.   2. Holocaust,
Jewish (1939–1945)—Poetry.   3. Lullabies, Yiddish—Translations
into English.   I. Kramer, Aaron, 1921–1997.   II. Lishinsky, Saul.
PJ5191.E3L37   1997
839'.11308—dc21   97-21242

Manufactured in the United States of America

With reverence and love
this collection is dedicated
to the poets of the ghettos
    and deathcamps
who left an indelible record
    of horror and glory
    and whose song
which kept them and their people defiant
    does indeed "go
like a signal through the years."

And

To the memory of Anna Weintraub—
To one who held these poems in her heart,
and these memories in her dreams.
May you, at last, sleep well.

Contents

Poets of the Holocaust

From Across the Wide Sea

Preface

Fifty years ago the death-camp gates were thrust open, revealing a horror that the world, including its revered leaders Churchill and Roosevelt, had murderously ignored. Endorsing the maxim that those who forget the past are doomed to repeat it, I have—with the encouragement of the Dora Teitelboim Foundation—gathered together my translations of Holocaust poetry. My translating began with two songs of the Vilna resistance ("Partisan Song" and "Ballad of Itzik Wittenberg"), done early in 1947, followed soon after by several poems that affected me deeply at the time, the work of dear friends much older than I and mostly now long dead—Sara Barkan, Shaye Budin, Ber Green, Isaac Ronch, Yuri Suhl, and Dora Teitelboim.

Throughout this half-century I have continued to render into English, at times obsessively, particularly stirring Holocaust pieces that have come my way. My major focus has been on those originally composed in Yiddish, because that language has fewer and fewer readers left, because that language was the mother-tongue of Hitler's chief victims, because that language—as Nobel Laureate Isaac Bashevis Singer reminded his Stockholm audience—was itself a victim and did not die a natural death but was murdered.

It is noble that a Holocaust museum now stands in the very capital city that was once the center of official failure to respond. It is noble that director Steven Spielberg devotes himself now to transmitting, on film and through Shoah interviews, the very imagery that screams forth from these pages. And not a moment too soon, for a powerful international conspiracy is just as energetically at work, encouraging the tendency to forget, to "let bygones be bygones," by denying that the Holocaust ever took place.

Even refugee friends have confessed to me that they never discuss among themselves or share with their children the atrocities that are their special inheritance: remembering is "too painful," and they want their loved ones to be spared the pain of knowing. As for me, despite the large number of Holocaust poems in my books, it has taken sixty years to confront, finally, the impact of Germany in 1935 on at least one child in Brooklyn:

"Mein Kind, wir waren Kinder"—Heine

My child, we three were children
in times of hunger and dread.
Our mothers pleaded and plotted
to bring us yesterday's bread.

And worse, because we were Jewish
in times of smashing and flames,
our dreams were of burning bedrooms,
of splintering window-panes.

It is no accident that this little ballad of 1995 also memorializes my beloved Heinrich Heine, the German master-poet whose books were then being burned (see N. D. Korman's "The Devils' Dance" on p. 231), and whose statue in Hamburg was melted down to make bullets.

If it is the poet's *nature* to remember, it is his or her *duty* to remind others. Not all of the poems that follow are great as art, but they are great as documents of humanity at its best, rejecting silent acquiescence in the face of brute force, and beautifully fulfilling the poet's duty to remind new generations of this genocide, and of all other genocides, so that the past will not be repeated.

It should go without saying, but let it be said at once, that although this collection focuses on Europe's Jews—the "problem" to which Hitler found a "final solution"—I have been alert all my life to earlier holocausts (who knows how many or where?) prior to recorded history, and, in more recent centuries, perpetrated against the indigenous peoples of Africa, America, and Australia. Nor have I been unaware of others systematically decimated by fascist force, even before *Kristallnacht,* such as the children of Guernica, and—throughout the war—the Gypsies.

The horrors recorded on the pages that follow are a metaphor for all the genocides of the past, witnessed by the world with—at best—

sympathetic paralysis. And despite the resolve rising from the Nuremberg trials never to permit a repetition of such monstrosity, the events depicted on these pages are at this writing being reenacted in the blood-soaked villages of Rwanda and Bosnia, universally characterized as akin to the Holocaust.

It is also appropriate to note here that, although the poets of this book are Jewish, non-Jews such as the Polish master Antoni Slonimski also raised their voices, in great nobility and power:

> They will not lie quiet;
> they will find breath
> to pass judgment on us
> who lived by their death.

And Bertolt Brecht's "Prayer of the Children" wrenches the heart half a century later:

> May fire not seize our homes.
> May no one hear of bombs.
> May night be only for sleeping.
> May life not be a whipping.
> May mothers not have to grieve.
> All children want to live.
> May everyone build together;
> then each could trust the other.
> May the young see this come true,
> the old people, too.

Acknowledgments

Of the many people who encouraged me in the creation of this book, I will here name only five: The Israeli editors and poets Benjamin Katz and Brache Kopstein, whose encouragement and guidance are evident in my lullabies; Rajzel Zychlinska, whose inspiration made a great impact on my translations of her work; Ber Green, for a lifetime of loyal friendship and inspiration and for six hours of intensive interviews that enriched my background in Yiddish literature; and Dina Abramowicz, YIVO's extraordinary librarian, whose caring has sparked my efforts and whose generous acts of service, far beyond the call of duty, merit my deepest gratitude. I especially thank my parents, Mary and Hyman Kramer who transmitted their love of Yiddish and their celebration of humanity at its best.

Many of these poems have hitherto appeared in *Bitterroot, Canadian Jewish Outlook, Chicago Jewish Forum, Jewish Currents, Jewish Life, Journal of Humanistic Psychology, Midstream, New England Review, Polish Review, Tikkun,* and *Visions.* Some of the volumes in which these poems can be found are *All My Yesterdays Were Steps: The Selected Poems of Dora Teitelboim, Anthology of Holocaust Literature, Anthology of Magazine Verse and Yearbook of American Poetry* (1985, 1988, and 1995 collections), *Apples and Honey, Blood to Remember, Canadian Jewish Outlook Anthology, A Century of Yiddish Poetry, "Jewish Life" Anthology, Kok Hameshamah, Ocarina: Freshness of the Ancient, The Right To Be Different, I. E. Ronch: Selected Poems, Songs of Peace, Freedom, and Protest, A Treasury of Jewish Folklore,* and *Warsaw Ghetto Uprising, April 19th, 10th Anniversary.*

The Dora Teitelboim Foundation

Dora Teitelboim, a distinguished poet in her own right, sought to promote Jewish secular culture by helping lesser-known Jewish poets and writers to get published in Yiddish and English. At the same time, she reached out to the lost generations of young Jews whose history, traditions, culture, and values had gone astray in the face of bewildering changes in today's world.

The foundation established in her name is dedicated to carrying on Dora Teitelboim's legacy by translating and publishing the works of Jewish writers, scholars, and poets the world over and by circulating them among Jewish cultural institutions, schools, organizations, and the public at large. Its explicit goal is to open a new world to the young by strengthening Jewish secular thinking, by promoting the teaching of Yiddish and the training of teachers, and by preserving and distributing important Yiddish works never before translated into English. In addition to publishing Yiddish works, the foundation anticipates the opening of a Jewish cultural center in the near future.

September 1996

DAVID WEINTRAUB
Executive Director

The Emperor of Atlantis
and Other Writings

Aaron Kramer

Creation in a Death Camp
(Based on the BBC script "Death Takes a Holiday")

"Those who were not there cannot possibly understand." Again and again, witnesses at the trials of death-camp officials say this. But the records—riskily scrawled, miraculously preserved—are now published, and the images of that horror-world have grown familiar. Each survivor of that hell is a wonder; that an opera should have been created, rehearsed, come close to performance, is almost beyond belief. But Terezin, or Theresienstadt, as its German masters called it, was unlike other camps.

On September 28, 1941, Reinhardt Heydrich came to power in Prague. Twelve days later, at a meeting attended by SS-Sturmbannführer Eichmann and other high officials, the fate of Czechoslovakia's Jews was decided. To help "evacuate the Jews from the Protectorate," Heydrich proposed using Terezin as a ghetto. Two to three trains containing a thousand Jews each could be sent every day. Straw would be allocated to the empty flats in the ghetto: "Beds would take up too much room. Let the Jews build flats under the earth."

A week later, at a second top-level meeting, Heydrich expanded his plan.

All armed forces will be completely evacuated from Theresienstadt. The Czechs will move elsewhere. Fifty to sixty thousand Jews may be comfortably accommodated. From there they will go East. After the complete evacuation of the Jews, the town will be settled by Germans and become a center of German life, in keeping with the ideas of the Reichs Commissar for the Propagation of German Culture. Under no account must any details of these plans become public.

The Jews of Prague suspected none of this. They eagerly believed the SS promises of a model Jewish city to be planned, built, and administered by a Council of Jewish Elders; a team of experts and workers would be sent there, and the families of these volunteers would not be transported to the East.

When Heydrich addressed the infamous Final Solution Conference at Wannsee on January 20, 1942, several death camps were already operating, and others were about to begin the extermination process Göring had called for the previous July. By then it had become clear, even to the most optimistic, that Terezin would be no final stop, no permanent refuge, for them. On January 9 and 15, the first two transports left Terezin for Riga. A thousand people were in each transport. They were driven—with numbers tied around their necks and carrying their packs—to the train and stuffed into the goods cars, seventy to ninety in a car.

But Terezin, the old fortress town in northern Bohemia, was to have a new and truly distinctive function: there would come Germany's oldest Jews and those seriously wounded in World War I, distinguished for war service. Interned there as well would be prominent German Jews with international connections, whose whereabouts might be questioned abroad. In a few months, the Potemkin village was ready to show Red Cross inspectors how benignly Germany treated its Jews. This device counteracted the ever-increasing rumors of atrocities at such places as Auschwitz and Buchenwald.

How could visitors guess that behind the Hollywood set was, in fact, nothing more than a detention center, a way station, a staging post through which the cream of Germany's Jewish intellectuals and artists were funneled into the gas chambers of Auschwitz? How could they imagine that, behind the scenes, Terezin's inhabitants lived in the most hideous filth and disease, many in huge, cold, airless attics where they perished by the thousands—33,430, to be precise, almost one fourth of the 139,606 who were sent there. No gas chambers were needed. Exhaustion, starvation, disease, and the whip did the job quite well. And overcrowding: Terezin had a population about fifty times greater than that of Berlin before the war.

But this the Red Cross did not see. The population density was solved before each of their visits. And those whose faces told of misery were first to vanish. What the Red Cross saw was a diabolic public relations diorama: make-believe shops, a bank that printed funny money, a coffeehouse, and a great deal of cultural activity. Thanks to Hitler's lootings, there was an impressive library—all but two of whose nineteen staff members were shipped east after the Red Cross visitors were gone. Like the rest of Terezin's cosmetic props, the library was shown in a film directed under protest by the Dutch Jew Kurt Gerron, formerly a well-known director and actor. For this public relations monstrosity, called *The Führer Presents the Jews with a City*, many pleasant activities were staged, including a symphony concert conducted by the once-famous Karel Ancerl, who now worked in the Terezin kitchen. The first act of *Tales of Hoffman* was also performed.

In fact, the SS did encourage artistic productions of an amazing variety—from cabaret entertainment to puppet shows to classical theater, including plays by Shakespeare, Shaw, and Molnar. Music was particularly supported, and opera flourished. On November 28, 1942, Smetana's *Bartered Bride* was performed; a half-demolished piano without feet substituted for an orchestra. The auditorium was the physical culture room in a home for boys. Still, it made an unforgettable impression. When the first bars, "Why should we not rejoice . . . ," sounded, there was not a dry eye in the house. That opera was done about thirty-five times. Its success was followed by Mozart's *Magic Flute* and *Marriage of Figaro*.

The Nazis preferred "safe" works. *Tosca, Aida, Carmen, La Bohème,* and *Die Fledermaus* were presented—some with simple piano accompaniment, some with orchestra and full staging. During 1943 and 1944, this activity was stepped up for the benefit of the Red Cross and other international agencies. In these *Stadtverschönerung,* or "window dressing" shows, the inspection teams found a remarkably high level of artistry, which is not surprising, because many of Europe's finest composers, vocalists, instrumentalists, and conductors were incarcerated there. Among them was the young Bohemian-born basso, Karel Berman, who, amazingly, survived.

"How often," he later reminisced, "did we sing out resistance and give the people strength to endure! We were indeed risking our necks when we sang 'The hour has struck—the gates are opening' from Smetana's *Brandenburg in Bohemia,* or, in Czech, the opera *In the Well,* though it was officially forbidden to speak Czech in public." On Czechoslovakia's national holiday, Berman offered a concert in the barracks, beginning with "O wicked time, the present time," from *In the Well,* continuing with such numbers as the aria from *Dalibor,* "You already know how this lovely kingdom has become the victim of wild passions."

Before 1939, at the Prague Conservatory, Raphael Schachter could find no better work than as assistant conductor. It was at Terezin that his true genius was recognized. From the time of his *Bartered Bride* production, he was acclaimed as the camp's foremost musician; artists competed to be in his ranks. He was allotted a little cellar room for rehearsals. There he revealed his great dream, to do Verdi's *Requiem*, realizing what the *confutatis maledictis,* and the *dies irae,* and the *libera me* would become, roared from Jewish throats in the pit of Hell itself.

For eighteen months this seemingly doomed effort gathered momentum, with the Terezin police themselves involved in smuggling score and music paper to the obsessed young conductor. Instrumentalists were also acquired somehow, and eventually an immense choir was being rehearsed—in segments, owing to lack of room. Often the rows were decimated as performers were removed to Auschwitz. Many felt the work would never have its premiere. They were astounded when Schachter announced that the commandant had pledged the company would henceforth remain intact.

That pledge turned out to be more diabolic in its subtlety than an outright act of violence. The musicians were spared, but not their families. Despite Schachter's pleading, many in the choir and orchestra, as well as three of his four superb soloists, elected to join their loved ones in the death transport. Those who remained had no heart for singing. But Schachter was more obsessed than ever. Once again he began the task of rebuilding. His rehearsals helped keep them alive from day to day. Other conductors pitched in; they lent him singers from their own projects: the brilliant Gideon Klein, working on *Rigoletto, Tosca,* and *Carmen,* and Fisher, preparing the oratorios *Elijah* and *The Creation.*

News from the outside seeped into Terezin: Hitler's military dream was disintegrating; his own cities smoked in ruin. For this reason, the genocide project was rushed toward completion. In June, the Lvov ghetto was liquidated. Through the summer, the Jews from Upper Silesia and elsewhere in Poland were transported to Auschwitz, and the Bialystok ghetto was wiped out. In September, Minsk and Vilna followed suit; by year's end, the Riga and remaining White Russian ghettos were empty. At this time the Danish Jews, along with those from southern France, northern Italy, and Rome, were deported. In the spring the Jews of Athens and Hungary were shipped—most to Auschwitz, which now had a capacity of ten thousand human bodies per twenty-four hours, and some to Terezin: artists, intellectuals, and others of international reputation among them.

The Verdi *Requiem* was finally done in early summer, and given a festive premiere in the committee room of the former town hall. On the platform stood the 150-member mixed choir, before them the soloists: Marion Podolier, Heda Aronson-Lindt, David Grunfelt, and Karel Berman, and in front on a little box stood Raphael Schachter, who knew the difficult score by heart. It was a revolutionary and militant feat that had no equal; an inspired performance, many said. The crowd, after a long silence, leaped to their feet with an ovation that could not seem to end. But Schachter was not satisfied. The conclusion struck him as too resigned. He wanted a *libera me* that would make the hair stand on end.

He revised Verdi's musical phrase, giving to those final words the Beethoven victory code: three short notes, one long. This new version was thundered from the stage at Eichmann and other dignitaries from Prague and Berlin later that summer. They had come, by Himmler's order, to bemedal the camp commandant of Terezin, which had played its special role so splendidly in achieving the final solution of the Jewish problem. It was told later that Eichmann applauded this "unique" interpretation of the *Requiem*.

But soon the summer ended. In September, the deportations from Slovakia were renewed and the last transport of French Jews left for Auschwitz. True to its pledge, the Terezin command did not separate Schachter's huge company. Together, on September 28, they climbed into the first wagons of the first transport, along with thousands of fellow inmates, including many Czech scientists and artists. They had known their fate the night before, when they gave the final performance of the *Requiem*.

The extraordinary cultural flowering at Terezin is hard to understand, but we must remember that the SS were, first of all, confident nothing heard here would ever reach the outside world; then too, they could not fathom the undermeanings of what was created and performed, such as Schachter's reworking of the *Requiem*, or a new interpretation of Mussorgsky's *Pictures at an Exhibition*. When the bells began to boom in "The Great Gate of Kiev," only the audience sensed the approach of the liberating Red Army.

What matters is the ferocious energy with which the inmates seized every opportunity to create original work. The most stunning example at Terezin—and perhaps in all history—of cultural defiance, is offered by Peter Kien and Viktor Ullmann, who created *The Emperor of Atlantis*, a one-act opera they described as "a legend in four scenes," with the subtitle *Death Abdicates*.

Of the librettist, a promising graduate student, we know little. He was born in 1919 in Varnsdorf, where his father owned a small textile factory. After Munich, the Kien family fled to the interior but was deported from there to Terezin in late 1941. Even as a child he had shown unusual versatility as a musician, poet, and especially as a graphic painter with a strong bent for caricature. He was an architect as well. A few hundred of Kien's drawings from his pre-Terezin years have been preserved. Several poems have also survived; these have been praised for a lyrical power as noteworthy as his graphic art. His photo reveals a handsome, wavy-haired young man with a wistful half-smile and bright, probing eyes behind glasses.

Of Ullmann, on the other hand, a good deal is known, thanks to the data in music encyclopedias. Born in Teschen on January 1, 1898, he studied with Schoenberg in Vienna in the early 1920s, became a theater conductor at Aussig, and was active as conductor and teacher in Prague before its fall to the Nazis. He was a founder-member of the Verein für Musikalisches Privataufführungen. His *Variations and Double Fugue on a Theme by Schoenberg* for orchestra were performed in 1929 at the Festival of the International Society for Contemporary Music in Geneva, one of his two string quartets was given at the 1938 London Festival, and other chamber works were heard at concerts of modern music in Europe and America. He wrote two operas—*Peer Gynt* and *The Fall of Anti-Christ*—as well as a wind octet, a piano concerto, and several song cycles. His style was atonal, but he adhered to the classical pattern in formal design.

At the death camp, Kien was one of a gifted group called "The Terezin Painters," who did their assigned poster work by day while secretly using their off-hours to record the hell around them. At least one formal exhibition of paintings by Kien and two colleagues was mounted. The other two, Fritta and Ungar, were arrested and fatally tortured when their clandestine work was discovered to have reached the outside world. As for Ullmann, probably encouraged by the presence of many outstanding performers and a sophisticated, music-hungry audience, he composed prolifically: seven piano sonatas, a string quartet, songs and choruses, and a melodrama based on Rilke's *The Lay of the Love and Death of Cornet Christoph Rilke*.

In terms of age and achievement, composer and poet seemed a strange pairing. But at Terezin age and temperament meant little. Survival was as much a requirement of the spirit as the body. Survival! that was the common denominator for all who rejected resignation, who refused to surrender the pulse of selfhood and turn into *Musselmänner*, walking corpses.

For Ullmann as composer, Terezin had been a transforming experience. From his opera it would be difficult to tell that he had been Schoenberg's pupil in Vienna. *The Emperor of Atlantis* gives a much stronger impression than his earlier work would lead one to expect. Here is a composer of depth and imagination, whose powerful musical and dramatic technique never masks his humanity. Humanity, yes, but no condescension, no oversimplification. The roles and the instrumental parts are extremely demanding; only an exceptional group of professionals could have coped with them; and the rich subtleties in the score could nourish the best-trained musical ear. But Terezin, where humanity fought hour by hour against the most heartless, technically brilliant onslaught ever known, was no place for the atonality he had acquired from Schoenberg. He arranged a group of Yiddish folksongs for the chorus. The tenderness and purity of those arrangements showed very clearly how his musical sympathies had shifted. Heydrich had declared him a Jewish rather than a Sudeten German composer; he knew now that he was both.

Having united their gifts for the creation of an opera, librettist and composer moved forward realistically. Singers and instrumentalists disappeared with each transport—so did large segments of their potential audience—so might they. It was necessary to shape a modest work: six singers could suffice, with the doubling of certain parts, plus two female dancers for the intermezzi and an orchestra of thirteen. Modest in length as well (less than an hour in performance time), it would follow a close-knit pattern of recitative and aria, molded at certain strategic points into vocal ensembles and punctuated twice by dance interludes.

With utmost modesty, *The Emperor of Atlantis* would declare itself a legend rather than an opera. Legends, parables can be rich with underlying significance yet on the surface be simple enough for a child to grasp and harmless enough to allay any suspicions of the camp guards: ruled by the Emperor Überall, Atlantis has become a land of horror. Declaring universal war, the Emperor patronizingly appoints his "old ally" Death to serve as standard-bearer. Death retaliates by breaking his sword: henceforth no one will be able to die. Two enemy soldiers, a boy and a girl, are commanded to fight to the death, but fall in love. As the forces of life advance against him, the Emperor begins to see that he has turned into a self-isolated monster. He begs Death to end his holiday, but Death insists that Überall be the first to die. As Death leads him away, the moral of the tale is given: Let us learn to respect the joy and pain of life, and not take the mighty name of Death in vain.

The elements of Kien's story were not unfamiliar. *Death Takes a Holiday* had recently been an international cinema hit, and through the centuries Death had been personified in parables and folk ballads of many cultures. Clearly, to us at least, the text is a thinly disguised satire on Hitler's despotic, psychotic, unprecedentedly arrogant and murderous career, which—as in the opera—was already collapsing by 1944. But it had to be more than a satire, more than a critique of absolute power. Probably their final say, it had to be large in scope and feeling, if not in cast and performance time. Not the Emperor, but Death, is the principal character—dignified, almost fatherly, as in Schubert's "Death and the Maiden." The Emperor insolently conceives of Death as his servant, an instrument for genocide. But Kien, at the very threshold of death himself, redefines its ancient and only proper function—as humanity's release from intolerable pain. Without Death, life is impossible, and with him he brings hope.

Ullmann's music translates whatever is in the text, whether elusive or sardonic. Clearly the master of many styles, he uses them—in the presence of a knowing audience—parodistically, to underscore a point or characterize a moment. The Emperor sounds Wagnerian. Death's aria about his glorious battles of the past is sung to a blues-like, saucy fox-trot step. For Pierrot's horror-lullaby, the composer borrows a grim children's tune from old Germany, "Maybug Fly." When the Drummer rolls out the Emperor's most pompous titles, such as Arch-Pope and King of Jerusalem, we hear an ironic paraphrase of "Deutschland Über Alles."

This tune had been used before to make a political statement. Carlo Taube had presented, in the prayer room of the "Magdeburg" barracks, a private premiere of his *Terezin Symphony.* The third movement had a shattering effect. His wife, Erika, recited, in a moving way, with a pianissimo obbligato from the orchestra, a lullaby of a Jewish mother, which she had written. There followed a turbulent finale in which the first four bars of "Deutschland Über Alles" were repeated over and over again, ringing out in more and more wrathful spasms, until the last outcry "Deutschland, Deutschland" did not continue to "Über Alles," but died out in a terrible dissonance. Everyone had understood and a storm of applause expressed thanks to Carlo and Erika Taube and all the musicians.

Such an audience, if not their jailers, would have savored the subtle irony of the Drummer's passacaglia, from the French *passe caille,* meaning goose-step. Just as the libretto starts out tantalizingly obscure and ends up deeply moving, so does the music, in the concluding hymn, paraphrase Bach's setting of Luther's "A Mighty Fortress Is Our God." But perhaps the most brilliant stroke by Ullmann and Kien is their use of the harmonium. This strange instrument was discovered in the old, abandoned church of Terezin, and the Nazis allowed it to be borrowed. Its metallic sound came as a kind of radio signal whenever the Emperor wanted to speak. What a comment on a mentality that glorified man's inhumanity to man!

The obtuseness of the camp officials had been demonstrated before. A Czech inmate, Hans Krasa, had revised and thoroughly reorchestrated for a Terezin production by orphan singers his hitherto unheard children's opera, *Brundibar.* It tells how a wicked organ grinder is finally defeated by the children of the town. A new ending was provided:

> Whoever loves justice
> and will defend it
> and is not afraid
> is our friend
> and may play with us.

Brundibar was a great success; it was done fifty-five times, including a command performance for the Red Cross visitors. Kien and Ullmann may very well have been inspired by its example.

Allegory and allusiveness have always been used as weapons of resistance by writers in times of repression. Malcolm Cowley reminds us that during World War II, nineteen issues of the militant journal *Poesie* somehow achieved legal publication in France: "This was possible because the collaborationist and German censors either did not scan its pages too closely, or were singularly thick-skulled and could not understand all its pointed barbs." If this could happen openly before the whole French population, one can hardly expect the commandant of Terezin to care much about the goings-on in a closely guarded camp from which no one was expected to escape alive. Besides, the Nazis at first saw nothing more than an innocuous tale.

The project may seem suicidal, but Kien and Ullmann worked with extreme prudence. They made two distinct versions of the libretto. The first, handwritten, has all the references to genocide and the power of the ruler. It is sharper and stronger than the second, the typewritten version submitted to the camp officials, which was probably typed for Kien by an SS officer, who used the backs of Terezin admission forms no longer of value because the inmates whose biographical data appeared on their pages had already been shipped to Auschwitz.

Karel Berman, the sole surviving participant, recalls the rehearsals "on the stage of the Sokol gymnasium. . . . Its tendency was so strongly antiwar that it was prohibited before it was ever performed. Specifically, the end of Hitler was the theme." Even on its most simplified nonallegorical and noncontroversial level, the plot should have been held suspect. But as allegory, the moral taught by Death defies the very core of Hitler's creed and career.

When Pierrot, the symbol of suffering humanity, asks Death to kill him because he can no longer make people laugh and life has become unbearable, Death declares: "No power on earth can kill you." How could the performers, and at last the censors, not translate this line to read: "The Nazis—any totalitarianism—have no ultimate power over mankind." When Death says: "The laughter that mocks itself is immortal," he obviously means: "The ability to laugh at yourselves in the face of your greatest agonies will help you survive."

The joyless, bloody world of Atlantis itself, no matter with how much universality Kien and Ullmann present it, bears too close a resemblance to Hitler's Europe. Most unacceptable of all is the Emperor's final recognition of Death's—and therefore Life's—supremacy over him. It would not do to show two enemy soldiers choosing love over war, singing: "Are there words on earth free of spite and hatred?" and defying the Emperor's exhortations by declaring: "No. Death is dead. Humanity need fight no more!" There was nothing innocuous about a parable ending with these lines: "Make us prize all human worth / to other lives awaken!" sung to a melody that definitively judges the Third Reich in terms of Germany's greatest spiritual voices —Luther and Bach.

It is unclear whether the work was well underway or rehearsals had just begun when the authorities forbade it to go on. As for its creators, they may indeed have been shipped to Auschwitz because of *Atlantis,* and almost as soon as the production of the opera was halted. But Terezin's musicians often participated in more than one project simultaneously. In mid-1944, many were transported to Auschwitz, including a large portion of Raphael Schachter's choir and orchestra, along with most of his soloists. Ullmann may have been among the thousands sent to the extermination center the morning after the September 27 performance of the *Requiem*. Certainly his singers were, and probably his instrumentalists as well. The circumstances of Peter Kien's death contradict the theory that Auschwitz was his punishment for having written the libretto. We know that he elected at the last minute to jump on the train carrying his parents to the gas chambers, and at twenty-five joined them in death.

It was long believed that the opera had been lost; but, along with other Ullmann pieces, it survived, smuggled out of the camp by a friend of the composer after Ullmann and Kien were dead. Apparently, the struggle for survival in the death camps involved not only the inmates but the written records of their captivity. We are not surprised to learn that in the ghetto of Lodz the superb poet Miriam Ulinover wrote prolifically, but none of her work survived the journey to Auschwitz's crematoria. What continues to amaze us is that when Vilna was liberated, partisans found a bloody bundle of Leib Apeskin's songs beside his body; that after the war several of partisan Jack Gordon's haunting poems were unearthed in the Bialystok ghetto; that the manuscript of Isaac Katzenelson's epic "Song of the Slaughtered Jewish People," along with other of his Yiddish poems in manuscript, was discovered in three hermetically sealed bottles in the hollow of an old tree in the Vittel camp from which he had been deported to Auschwitz. We read of the unbelievable care taken, at extreme risk and with breathtaking ingenuity, by the partisan-poets Avrom Sutzkever and Shmerke Katcherginsky to preserve not only themselves and their writings, but every piece of ghetto and death-camp poetry they could get their hands on, as well as a priceless treasury of Jewish culture in Vilna, sought by Hitler, which they hid in a bunker until the end of the war.

The English-language version of *Atlantis,* in my translation, finally received its premiere at the San Francisco Opera in April 1977. On opening night, many in the audience stood in tears after a phenomenal number of curtain calls. The central issue of this work's intrinsic merit, aside from the circumstances of its creation, cannot be ignored. As one critic has written, "A knowledge of the conditions which produced the opera adds an extra emotional resonance, but it would stand as a powerful theatre piece even if it were possible to detach it from its tragic background." In *Time Magazine,* reporting the Amsterdam premiere, Lawrence Malkin asked: "Confronted by a vision of hell, does one stand in silent reverence for the suffering or praise the spirit that surmounted it? Last week a Dutch audience faced this dilemma. At the end, after a few seconds' pause, the listeners burst into applause for a work that stands on its own as a music drama of great power." Perhaps Hubert Saal of *Newsweek* put it best: "It is incredible that in the hell where they were confined, Ullmann and Kien retained the will to create. They speak to us like dying men whose last words cannot be denied. Amazingly, they were able to convert their own agony into a universal, hypnotically theatrical drama."

Obviously, objective judgment is not easy, and it may take a long time before *The Emperor of Atlantis* can be accurately gauged as art; but there is no question of its uniqueness as an affirmation of the human spirit in the teeth of physical obliteration. Perhaps it was by the very act of creation that both men survived almost until the end of the Holocaust. The same can be said of the audience for whom it was created. Karel Berman recalls:

> If the historians one day succeed in writing the cultural history of the ghetto of Terezin, mankind will be amazed. Grown-ups and children, in constant expectation of death, lived a full, noble life, between outcries of pain and anxiety, among the "mussulmen"—those more dead than alive; in hunger and misery, among the hundreds of corpses of those that died daily, among hearses taking the corpses out of town and bringing back bread, under constant great physical exertion, they lived a life that was a miracle under the given conditions.

After the collapse of France a few years earlier, the supreme Resistance poet Louis Aragon had written: "It takes a great deal of courage to write without knowing what will happen to one's work." Yes—but what joy it must have given this composer and his young librettist to have found a vehicle worthy of their awesome theme, and to have achieved its completion with sustained artistic integrity. On May 25, 1941, under the Nazi heel, a strangely exhilarated Aragon wrote of his reawakened purpose: "With the greatest freedom of expression we said nothing—magnificently. And now we have found what we had to say, more than we had ever dreamed. Can we say it well enough?"

Surely this was the challenge and the glory experienced by Viktor Ullmann and Peter Kien as their opera took shape.

The Emperor of Atlantis

Viktor Ullmann and Peter Kien

1. PROLOGUE

LOUDSPEAKER. Hello, hello! This work is called: "Death Abdicates" —a sort of opera in four scenes. The characters include Emperor Overall in person, who hasn't been seen for some years; he shut himself away in his giant palace, totally isolated, so that he might rule better; the Drummer, whose appearance is not quite real, like a radio; the Loudspeaker, whom one hears but does not see; a Soldier and a Girl, in the third scene; Death, as a discharged soldier; and Pierrot, who can laugh in spite of his tears: that's life.

The first scene takes place somewhere; Death and Pierrot sit at the borderline of a living that can no longer laugh, and a dying that can no longer cry, in a world that has forgotten how to enjoy life while living and how to achieve death when dying. Death, who has been repelled and offended by the hustle and bustle, the speed, and the technological developments of modern life, breaks his sword to teach mankind a lesson, and decides that from now on he will allow no one to die! Hello, hello! We're beginning!

Scene 1

2. PRELUDE

3. PIERROT'S SONG

PIERROT.   The moon on stilts is skirting
the rooftops of the town;
the young are thirsting
for love and wine.
The moon, despite their yearning,
takes both away: there's no returning
—love nor wine returning.

So what are we to drink now?
Blood, is what we'll drink now.

15

Death

And what are we to kiss now?
The Devil's backside.
The world's all topsy-turvy now
and whirling like a carousel;
and we are forced to ride.

The moon is white
and blood is hot;
the wine is sweet
and love has gone to Paradise.
In this poor world, then, what's our share?
We'd sell our souls at the nearest fair.
Will nobody buy us?
Will nobody buy us?
Since each man wants to be rid of himself,
we must go wherever the four winds drive us.

4. RECITATIVE AND DUET

DEATH. No more. What song was that?

PIERROT. Oh, just a song . . .

DEATH. Well, tell me what day it is today?

PIERROT. I've stopped keeping track of days as I used to, since I've got no shirt to speak of, and will not take up a new day till I've got some fresh, clean underwear.

DEATH. Then you must be deep in months that are long gone by.

PIERROT. Perhaps Tuesday? Wednesday? Friday? Each is like the other.

DEATH and PIERROT.
One day, two days,
who'll buy new days?
Lovely, fresh days, undiscovered;
each is like the other.
Perhaps one of them will bring good luck;
you'll be a king then!
Who'll buy new days?
Who'll buy old days? Buy one!
Old days cheaper, come try one!

5. RECITATIVE AND ARIA

PIERROT. From the day I first looked with loathing on myself, there's been a sickness deep inside me. I wish you would kill me; it's your profession, after all—and I am so bored, every moment's unbearable!

DEATH. Leave me in peace; no power on earth can kill you. The laughter that mocks itself is immortal. You're still yourself; there's no escaping. What you are is Pierrot!

PIERROT. And what is that? Only a memory, paler than all the yellowed photographs of these wretched creatures who can smile no longer. I get laughs from no one . . . If I could just forget what young wine tastes like! If once more the long-forgotten touch of a woman could stir my being . . .

6. RECITATIVE AND ARIA

DEATH. Ridiculous! It makes me laugh when I hear you. You're scarcely three hundred years old, and I, I've been part of this theater ever since time was! Now I am old and cannot keep up . . . If only you'd seen me back there!

They had such wars then! The most spectacular clothes were worn to pay me homage! Gold and purple, glittering coats of mail . . . They decked themselves for me the way a bride prepares for her consort. Colorful banners fluttering over the cavalry . . . Foot-soldiers rolled out their dice on the battle-drum; and when they danced, the bones of the women would crack—they were wet from the sweat of their partners . . . So often I raced beside the little horses of Attila as they galloped! *And* ahead of Hannibal's elephants, and the tigers of Djehangir—that my old legs are so weary they can no longer follow the motorized legions of fighters. What can I do now but limp in the wake of Death's new battalions of angels, a lowly tradesman of dying? (*The Drummer appears behind the fence and issues a proclamation.*)

7. RECITATIVE

DRUMMER. Hello, Hello! Attention. Attention, please! In the name of his Majesty, the Emperor Overall. By the grace of God, we, Overall the Glorious, pride of the Fatherland, blessing to mankind . . . ruler of

Lovers

Pierrot's Inferno

both Indies, Emperor of Atlantis, Imperial Duke in the land of Ophir, High Priest of Astarte, Ban of Hungary, Cardinal-Prince of Ravenna, King of Jerusalem, and—to glorify our divine descent from God—Arch-Pope . . . have, in our flawless, truly perfect, all-penetrating wisdom, decided to declare, through all our lands, total, God-inspired War! Each against the other! To the finish!

8. ARIA

DRUMMER. Every child, both male and female; every maiden, wife and mother; every man, deformed and able-bodied—shall now carry weapons in this holy crusade, which must end in victory for our most apostolic Majesty, and the destruction of wickedness in our dominions.

And as you hear these words, we proclaim our campaign triumphantly opened. Our old ally, Death, will lead the way with his glorious banner, in the name of our great future and his great past. Fight bravely! Decreed in the fifteenth year of our prosperous reign. Signed: Emperor Overall!

DEATH. Hear that? Hear how they mock me? It's only I who can take men's souls! My banner lead the way! My great past! Your great future! Big Shot!

PIERROT. Ha-ha, ha-ha!

DEATH. *(Draws his sabre as Drummer exits, repeating the proclamation.)* Hi-hi! In the name of your great future!

PIERROT. What are you doing?

DEATH. I'm making the future of mankind great—and long . . . long!!

CURTAIN

LOUDSPEAKER. From his office, the Emperor of Atlantis communicates with his ministers by telephone and radio. Following the execution of several prisoners, he realizes that Death has decided to stop working. People cannot die; the old and the sick are doomed to endure the throes of death forever. The Emperor tries to prevent the panic this news must bring; he tells his subjects they will be liberated by Death's abdication: set free from a tyranny that till now has subjugated every living creature.

9. DANCE-INTERMEZZO: "THE DANCE OF DEATH"

Scene 2

10. RECITATIVE AND ARIA

The empty imperial palace.

EMPEROR. What time is it?

LOUDSPEAKER. Five thirty-two. Hello, hello. Royal guard reporting, sentry commander. The cordon 'round the palace has been tripled as ordered.

EMPEROR. Armed and ready?

LOUDSPEAKER. Armed and ready.

EMPEROR. Good.

LOUDSPEAKER. Hello, hello! Assaulting battalions, dive-bombers, underground torpedos have demolished the ramparts surrounding our third largest city. The inhabitants are dead. Corpses have been delivered to the recycling plant.

EMPEROR. How many?

LOUDSPEAKER. Ten thousand kilos of phosphorus.

EMPEROR. Fine! The Ministry!

LOUDSPEAKER. Hello, hello. Ministry.

EMPEROR. The execution?

LOUDSPEAKER. Performed as commanded at four-thirteen.

EMPEROR. Well then, are they dead?

LOUDSPEAKER. Death's certain to come any moment now!

EMPEROR. What? Certain to? When was the sentence carried out?

LOUDSPEAKER. Four-thirteen.

EMPEROR. But it's now five thirty-five!

LOUDSPEAKER. Death's certain to come any moment now!

EMPEROR. Have you lost your senses? Has the hangman, in an hour and twenty-two minutes, failed to kill them?!

LOUDSPEAKER. Death's certain to come any moment now!

EMPEROR. *(Jumps up.)* Am I mad? Have I gone crazy? Are they wrestling death away from me? Who in the future still will fear me? *(Leaves his desk.)* Does Death refuse his duty? Has he smashed his ancient sabre? Who now will give allegiance to the Emperor of Atlantis?—Hello! Fill them with bullets!

LOUDSPEAKER. Performed as ordered.

The Great Leader

EMPEROR. Well?!

LOUDSPEAKER. Death's certain to come any moment now.

EMPEROR. What?!—The Doctor!

LOUDSPEAKER. Hello, doctor speaking.

EMPEROR. Well?

LOUDSPEAKER. He's still alive. A very strange sickness has broken out. People can't die.

EMPEROR. Is it such a bad thing that people can't die? How many have died since the epidemic began?

LOUDSPEAKER. None. Thousands, mortally wounded, are grappling with life so that they can die.

EMPEROR. Thank you. Issue commands. Ministry! Posters on every corner. Special announcements on the radio. Drummers in the villages: We, Overall the Glorious, give to all our deserving citizens a secret formula for life everlasting. He who possesses it shall be safeguarded from death, and neither sickness nor any injury can henceforth stop him from carrying the sword of his fatherland and his master. Death, where is thy sting? Where's thy victory, Hell?!

LOUDSPEAKER. A man and a girl, from the two enemy camps, confront each other, brandishing weapons. The news that people are unable to die transforms their war-like spirit into love. Instead of killing one another, they embrace. The Drummer tries in vain to persuade the man to follow him.

Scene 3

11. RECITATIVE AND DUET

SOLDIER. Who's there?

GIRL. Halt! Stop! Who's there?

SOLDIER. A man.

GIRL. Yes, but a foe!

DRUMMER. "Give to all our deserving citizens a secret formula for life everlasting . . ."

SOLDIER. Such lovely skin!

GIRL. Shoot! Why don't you?

DRUMMER. ". . . shall be safeguarded from death . . ."

SOLDIER. In my young days, I would sometimes walk with a girl and stroll beside the river. She had eyes that were bright, like yours!

GIRL. I'm not yet old enough to have such moments to remember

. . . Hear him calling!

DRUMMER. ". . . Death, where is thy sting? Where's thy victory, Hell?!"

SOLDIER. Heavy weapons, steel adornments, press upon your tender flesh! Girl, you should endure no torments; see, the world is bright and fresh.

12. ARIA OF THE GIRL

GIRL. Is it true? Are there landscapes on earth, free of blight and parchedness? And say—are there words on earth free of spite and harshness? And say—are there fields on earth full of brightness and fragrance? Is it true? Are there hills on earth that shimmer blue in the radiance?

13. RECITATIVE, ARIA, AND TRIO

DRUMMER. You must not stay; come go with me! Go with me!

GIRL. You must not stay; come go with me! Come away!

DRUMMER. Both King and Duty bid you fight!

GIRL. We're beckoned by the distant light . . .

DRUMMER. You're called to death; you're called to war.

GIRL. No, Death is dead; Humanity need fight no more!

DRUMMER. (*Alluringly.*) The wardrum, wardrum whines and pounds; a man can't help but be lured by its sounds. For its skin is smooth, its feel is warm, and rounded like a woman's form. It speaks a language loud and full. A man must follow at its call!

GIRL AND SOLDIER. We see what makes fair even Death's grim face: the flower of love that inspires us to embrace. (*Drummer exits.*)

14. DUET OF SOLDIER AND GIRL

See, the sullen clouds that hovered have been lifted from our sight, and the landscape, grayly covered, suddenly is bathed in light. Deepest shadows turn to fire at the rising of the sun. Death takes up the poet's lyre now that he and Love are one.

15. DANCE INTERMEZZO: "THE LIVING DEAD"

LOUDSPEAKER. Because of Death's refusal to let the people die, the Emperor witnesses a total collapse of society. The sick are terrified at being robbed of deliverance from their pain, and a chaotic madness has set in. The Emperor, too, is seized by the universal excitement; long-forgotten impressions from his childhood emerge, embodied by Pierrot. However, the Drummer tries to inspire him to hold firm. In conflict with himself, the Emperor has a vision. Death steps out of the mirror; he regrets the suffering his abdication has caused, and is ready to return to mankind; but the Emperor must agree to be the first to suffer the new death. The Emperor of Atlantis agrees, and humanity, redeemed, greets the return of Death.

Scene 4

LOUDSPEAKER. Hello, hello, Supreme General here: Hospital 34 for the Living Dead was captured by the rebels at three o'clock. Doctors and instructors surrendered en masse. The insurgents carry black flags and display a bloody plough on their coat of arms. They fight without a battle-cry, silent and bitter. The General Staff of the 12th Army has not yet submitted its report.

EMPEROR. What else?

LOUDSPEAKER. That is all!

EMPEROR. Good! Hello, Ministry! Which headquarters have fallen into the hands of the rebels?

LOUDSPEAKER. 57-3-Roman VIII, 120-Roman XXXII/1/10/11B.

EMPEROR. Is the proclamation printed?

LOUDSPEAKER. Printed and dispatched.

EMPEROR. Yes.

LOUDSPEAKER. *(Another headquarters reporting.)* An awesome surgeon has removed the cataract from our eyes and healed us of our blindness; great as the madness of our sins is the punishment, frightful the anguish we must endure. Let us bear it with humility, and never rest till we've rooted out of our hearts the last rank weed of hate and disharmony. With bare hands we shall tear down the tyrant's steel ramparts . . .

16. RECITATIVE AND ARIA

EMPEROR. Has no one else died? No sick, old, wounded?

LOUDSPEAKER. No one.

EMPEROR. I can hardly believe it. I'm getting all mixed up. Once we were children . . .

PIERROT. We skipped to the candy store for chocolate and peppermint; we dreamed that one day we'd be stars of the circus tent. We often used to ride the hobby-horse together! We sledded on our schoolbags in snowy weather. Before the gaze of little girls we quaked and quivered. We shattered injustice with pure thoughts—and the world was delivered!

DRUMMER. "We Overall, we Overall, the world is full of all our doing. Go if you dare, no matter where, we'll meet you there, and be your ruin. Sense is but nonsense, wisdom but a fool—We Overall."

PIERROT. Bye, lullaby, an epitaph am I. Your father perished in the war, your mother's red mouth finished her, bye, lullaby. Sleep, baby, sleep; the man in the Moon doth reap. He reaps our joy, he cuts the crop, and in the sun it all dries up. You'll put your little red dress on then, and start the same old song again. Bye, lullaby . . .

17. MAD TRIO

EMPEROR. Five, six, seven, eight, nine, ten, hundred, thousand bombs, and how many million cannon . . .

DRUMMER and PIERROT. Don't you worry, don't you worry.

EMPEROR. I hid behind my formidable walls without windows. This item also was in my calculations! . . . But what are men like?

DRUMMER. For years he kept the mirror concealed!

EMPEROR. Can I be called a man, or just the adding machine of God?

DRUMMER and PIERROT. Am I a man? *(The Emperor pulls down the sheet; behind the mirror stands Death. Overall recoils and draws his gun.)*

DRUMMER and PIERROT. A living dead man. Ha-ha-ha . . .

DEATH. There's nothing you can do to me. I've been dead since the beginning of time.

EMPEROR. Who are you?

18. DEATH'S ARIA

DEATH. I'm known as Death, the Gardener Death; I sow the seeds of sleep in pain-cut furrows. I'm known as Death, the Gardener Death; I pull pale weeds exhausted after many morrows. Men call me Death, the Gardener Death; and in the fields I reap the ripened corn of sorrows.

I'm not the Plague that brings you pain; I bring relief. I'm not the one who tortures men, but he who soothes their grief.

I am the comfortable, warm nest to which an anguished life at last can fly. I'm freedom's festival, the last and best. I am the final lullaby. Hushed is my house and glad to greet each guest . . . Come, take your rest.

EMPEROR. Then you'll come back to us? Without you we people could not live.

DEATH. I'll come back if you agree to be the first to die.

EMPEROR. I have the courage to make this sacrifice. But the people don't deserve it . . .

DEATH. In that case I can't return to you.

EMPEROR. Should I refuse what all who suffer beg of you? . . . I'll do it.

DEATH. Give me your hand. The war is over.

EMPEROR. The war is over?

19. THE EMPEROR'S FAREWELL

EMPEROR. The war is over. So you say with pride. No other war has stopped, no war but this. The last one? White banners fluttering, from every tower the bells sound forth their festive tidings; and the fools will all come dancing, singing, leaping. Ah, but how long will there be peace? The flame is merely weakened, not put out. It soon will blaze anew. Once more shall murder rage, and I yearned to share the grave's repose! O were my task accomplished! Freed from these fetters forged by man, the land would stretch in golden realms of unploughed meadows. Ah, were we turned to dust! The wilds which we have maimed would bloom forever! None would tame the roaring of a mighty river. Death would come as hunger, love and life come: sometimes slowly or swift as lightning—but never to slay! Into your hand we place our life; lead me away, lead me away, lead me away. *(Death takes the Emperor gently by the hand and leads him off.)*

20. FINALE

GIRL, DRUMMER, PIERROT, and LOUDSPEAKER.

Come, Death, our worthy, honored guest,
into our hearts descending.
Lift all life's burdens from our breast;
lead us to rest,
our sorrows ending.

Make us prize all human worth
to other lives awaken.
Let this commandment be our truth:
The great and sovereign name of Death
must not be lightly taken!

CURTAIN

Janne Furch-Allers

You, Who're Permitted to Live . . .
(For Anne Frank)

You, who're permitted to live—can you hear my quiet step in all
this hullabaloo?
Within the shadow of each summer-cloud my shadow wanders too
and settles on blossoming valleys, on rivers,
on children at play, on graves and on gleaming guns—
you, who're permitted to live, will you care for the freedom
and life of another man's sons?

You, who're permitted to live—do you know the wherefore of love?
Are you prepared to give it to the next one, the poor one,
the cripple, the stranger, the one who is different from you?—
You, who're permitted to live, did love die with me too?

D'you hear? Are you able to hear me
in the wind's inconsolable sighing?
in the scream of the bird that fell from its nest?
Somewhere a child has been abandoned:
can you hear me in its crying?

You, who're permitted to live, do you see Earth's majesty?
the springtime, the creatures, the mountains, the sheen of the stars,
the spear of grass, that thrusts through pavement,
the thousand wonders I never again shall thrill to and nevermore see.

You, who're permitted to live, are you thankful to Heaven therefor?
To the voices of the dead do you sometimes open your door?

Many are merely leaves, soon lost in the moldering heap.—
But I must be flame, must be fire and light
in the hearts of the living to leap!

Lullabies of the Holocaust

Lullabies of the Holocaust

My source for most of these lullabies is *Unter Yankele's Vigele* (*Under Yankel's Cradle,* Tel Aviv, 1976), a valuable anthology edited by the fine Canadian-Israeli poets Benjamin Katz and Brache Kopstein, whose enthusiastic support helped bring these translations into being. An excerpt of their introduction deserves to be quoted here (the English is mine):

> What is a lullaby? A lullaby should cradle, quiet, calm, and bedrowse the child . . . at dusk, when the sun sets, when day ends, and a full-fed, well-bathed baby lies in a tidy cradle, rocked with a tale of gold and silver. The Yiddish lullaby, from Goldfaden on, depicts a widow who sits cradling her child with a song: "My little Jew will ride forth to sell raisins and almonds." The motif and all the properties of the little goat, of "prayers" being "the best wares," that recur in a great many Yiddish lullabies, is not a quieting song but the heavy heart of a mother, that unlocks itself to her little orphan and dreams of his future.
>
> Yiddish lullabies are not slumber-songs but awakening-songs, terror-songs, battle and fury-songs, filled with social storm and stress; and the cradle has become a non-cradle—no longer is there a home; the open field is now home, in a no-man's land besieged by war, in ghettos and concentration-camps—the whole ravaged Jewish life is reflected in tens of lullabies. The upgathered rage and woe: "I could / have poisoned with my milk this planet / and left no live thing on it," Hadassah Rubin sings; and not one Yankele is lulled: "Help me, mothers, help me / rock Babi-Yar to rest!" pleads Shike Driz.

My own anthology, *A Century of Yiddish Poetry,* includes only one lullaby. It is by Leah Rudnitsky, an already well-known young poet who joined a partisan unit in the woods outside Vilna, a major cultural center on which the panzers had pounced with lightning speed, and who survived as a warrior until her capture in 1943. Like several others, her eerie cradlesong presents "a stranger / singing lullabies" to an infant "whose mother / never will come back."

There is a certain surrealism, almost a wildness, in the scores of Holocaust lullabies I have translated. This is an ancient tradition, going back to the Inquisition and later periods of pogroms, and—through the imagination of a classic late-nineteenth century Yiddish writer,

I. L. Peretz—back to Egypt itself, in a dearly loved lullaby sung by Jochebed to her infant son, Moses.

In the latest horror-epoch especially, it was the vast scope of nightmarish situations that inspired such an assortment of approaches. Sometimes it was the father who took up his dead wife's melody. There are lullabies to murdered children and to others who will never be born; to a doll (sung by a little girl whose parents are dead); to a stone; to children snug in their New York beds; to empty or vanished cradles. A new reason emerged to make the hungry child—robbed of father, siblings, and home—stop crying:

> Hear me, child—the sentry hovers
> near us, so don't cry!
> He might shoot, if he discovers
> someone didn't die.

In the 1944 Terezin opera *The Emperor of Atlantis* (see p. 15) Pierrot wishes to die because the people in their misery can no longer laugh at him. Near the end he sings a wild cradlesong to the orphans of war, who once "skipped to the candy store for chocolate and peppermint":

> Bye, lullaby,
> an epitaph am I.
> Your father perished in the war,
> your mother's red mouth finished her,
> bye, lullaby.

A century before, during the turbulence preceding the 1848 revolutions in Central Europe, the great German-Jewish poet Heinrich Heine struck a similarly wild note in his marvelous lullaby "Charles I," imagining the soon-to-be-beheaded British monarch rockabying the infant destined to be his headsman:

> My death-song is your cradle-song—
> lullaby-lulla—the old
> locks of my hair you'll cut off first;
> at my throat the iron rings cold.
>
> Lullaby-lulla, what stirs in the straw?
> You shall not be denied.
> You'll take the empire, and cut off my head—
> the pussycat has died.

Among the creators of the songs that follow are some unknown or little-known Holocaust victims as well as several who achieved fame (Shmerke Katcherginsky, Isaiah Spiegel, Leizer Wolf) and one, Avrom Sutzkever, who towers over the rest as not only a great resistance hero but also a great world-poet. Several fine Soviet Yiddish poets are also represented (Moishe Broderson, Shike Driz, Itzik Feffer). Along with this group are quite a few who from overseas expressed their sense of horror in unforgettable verses; these include such master-poets as Jacob Glatstein, Zische Landau, H. Leivick, Itzik Manger, Mani-Leib, Kadia Molodowsky, and Melech Ravitch.

But perhaps the most touching Holocaust lullaby (composed in German, as were "Charles I" and *The Emperor of Atlantis*) is by a seventeen-year-old girl from Czernowicz, inmate of a concentration camp near the Bug River, who perished a year later, in 1942.

How Selma Meerbaum-Eisinger must have hungered for the tenderness of her vanished mother, how that voice must have echoed within her, for such a wildness—a lullaby to oneself!—to burst from her at last in the very precincts of death:

> I sing me and sing, in the midst of my woe,
> the song of good hope and good luck;
> I sing it like someone who still doesn't know
> for him there is no turning back.
>
> I tell me and tell me that lovely old tale
> of living and loving entwined;
> and though I keep saying it over, I feel
> how different a fate will be mine.

Because I feel strongly that the focus in the pages that follow should be on the lullabies rather than the poets, the biographical data (where there are any) will be given at the end of the section. The poems are clustered according to theme: children safe in their American beds; children wandering, hunted, in despair; motherless children; child and doll; dead children, empty cradles; children inspired by their Jewishness; fathers fighting, with a sense of defiance and ultimate victory.

Melech Ravitch

A Cradlesong For American-Jewish Children—1940

Sleep, my child, my Jewish child;
there's no fear, no grief to hound you.
Yes, your sleep is quiet, darling,
in New York, with full two million
fellow Jews around you.

Sleep, my beautiful. Turn over,
face the wall, and while you slumber
I've a ballad about children
in a far-off land to sing you—
brothers without number.

Sleep, my child; the land is Poland;
and those brothers, sisters—never
have you seen them, though they're blood of
your blood, bone of your bone, nor shall
see them, though you searched forever.

You've got aunts there too, and uncles;
grandpas hunched, with gray beards flowing;
more great-grandpas in the ground than
can be counted; grandmas also—
eyes no longer glowing.

Sleep, my child; throughout that country
flash of sword is to be found now,
and your brothers and your sisters
pick, like sparrows gnawed by hunger,
nibblings from the ground now.

Sleep, my child; throughout that country
graves, like grass, are multiplying;
and in snow, in wind, in rain there
with no roof but heaven above them,
orphan lads are lying.

Drive them from your dream, my darling—
sleep, your People's gold adornment!
If there's dreaming, let your sisters
and your brothers dream of you, who
have not tasted torment.

Sleep, my child, you brightest flower
of our Tree—why feel so frantic
for your brother, sister branches
drooping blighted on the other
side of the Atlantic?

Sleep, my child, it's night; above you,
wrapped in cloud, he too is sleeping—
God, the grandfather who loves you.—
Sleep, then. You're in New York's keeping;
sleep—no fear, no weeping;
sleep—

I've put out the light, and God has
locked the wind inside its stable.
Hush. The song is also finished.
You may really sleep now, Jewish
child—if you are able.

Mani-Leib

Night and Rain

Husha-husha, night and rain,
husha-husha, night and storm.
In the night and in the rain
in the night and in the storm
people pass through road and lane
homeless, hungering, forlorn;
drenched like homeless dogs, forlorn.

Husha-husha, night and rain,
husha-husha, night and storm.
Sleep you, safe and warm!

Would you know where they are going?
Ask the night and ask the storm.
No one screaming, no tears showing
in the night and in the storm
ranked in rows forever flowing
drenched like dogs they go, forlorn,
driven, hungering, forlorn.

Husha-husha, night and rain,
husha-husha, night and storm.
Sleep you, safe and warm!

Kehos Kliger

The Last Cradlesong

Child, on the other side of the door
our rest awaits us, we'll quake no more;
a blue, a heavenly rest; don't cry,
shut forever your angel-eye—
husha, hushabye.

Child, on the other side of the wall
the ghetto is done with, once and for all;
somewhere a bird will sing in the sky,
shut forever your angel-eye—
husha, hushabye.

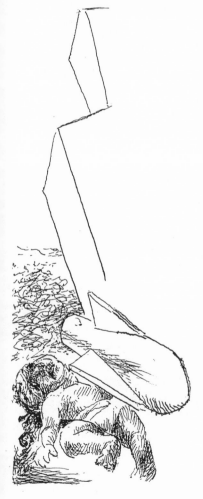

Child, on the other side of the town
no guns, no charged wire can be found;
we'll dream a long time, you and I,
shut forever your angel-eye—
husha, hushabye.

Child, on the world's other side
nothing you crave will be denied;
cornbread, cow's milk, pudding and pie,
shut forever your angel-eye—
husha, hushabye.

Child, on the other side of the door
our rest awaits us, we'll quake no more;
a deep, a god-long rest; don't cry,
shut forever your angel-eye—
husha, hushabye.

Isaiah Spiegel

Ghetto Lullaby

Time now to shut your eyes;
out of the darkening skies
come birds, and at your cradle's head they fly about.
The house is ash and brands—
with bundle in our hands
in search of shelter, darling, we set out.

The world's been bolted down,
and night is all around—
prepared to pounce with horror and with woe.
A wretched pair, we cower
here in a grim, grim hour
and where our path may lead we do not know.

They drove us, naked, forth
to wander south and north.
Into the fields of midnight we were hurled;
and hailstorms, blizzards wild
have followed you, my child,
followed you to the precipice of the world.

Bezalel Friedman

Lullaby

No pillow for your weary head,
no walls to keep you warm . . .
sleep, my naked little one,
upon your mother's arm . . .

Don't cry, my love, in no-man's land!
Your tear chokes me alone . . .
The eye of man is blind, my babe,
his ear is deaf as stone!—

Your father, from behind barbed wire,
sends you a soft embrace.
Sleep, my unsheltered baby, with
no roof, no resting-place.

Shut your precious eyes and sleep
amid the winds and guns . . .
Mother's tear, her bitterest,
down your forehead runs.

Benjamin Katz

Wandersong

Wander, cradle, up and wander!
In the west the sun goes under.
Night descends on us, my dear;
who was it that brought us here?

Driven from home, each night we stay
somewhere, and are gone by day.
What's our fate to be tomorrow?
Sleep, child, sleep away your sorrow.

In the woods howl wolf and wind;
drenched with dew, the grasses bend.
Drenched with dew are mothers' eyes.
Who will hearken to our cries?

—Wind nor frost! Against the world
howlings of the storm are hurled.
But it cannot thus remain;
sleep, child, sleep away your pain.

Sleep, my love; Zbonzin is near.
All are being driven there.
Wander, cradle, wake and run!
Nazi-demons drive us on.

Zische Landau

A Cradlesong for Today

Overhead a cold moon gleams;
drowse, my darling, into dreams.
Night gives none of us repose—
time, lad, for your eyes to close.

In expectancy and fright
we endure the day, the night.
In the chimney something wails—
but it's not November's gales.

Not for starving wolves arise
far off those beseeching cries.
Lad! like stone, without a sound,
German prowlers roam around,

spreading darkness, sowing fears,
making sharp their glowing spears.
Even babes they do not spare;
Death goes with them everywhere.

And whoever comes their way
shall not see another day.

Ricudah Potash

The Moon Is Going to Sleep

The moon is tired of shining,
my child.—
She's going to sleep;
she comes from the coasts of the sea
where the refugees lie
and weep.

The moon is going to sleep,
my child.—
She scouted about, but found
no nest where the refugees
would not have to sleep on the bare
silver ground.

The moon is going to sleep,
my child.—
The heart within her
has split in two.
She's just come riding, over
seas with the woe of the Jew.

The moon is going to sleep,
my child,—
and red with rage is she;
her head lies in a cloud now,
like a drowsing refugee.

Kadia Molodowsky

Three Children

Three children, three wretched
worms, are aslumber,
worn out—by the death of their mother,
by crawling in autumn water
amid graves without number.

Their lips, their young lips parted,
night has cradled asleep
these heavy-hearted,
concealed the dark mound
and filled the hollows;
only their pain is sleepless;
it bothers their eyelids,
cramps their knees,
and in their dreams it bellows.

A white moon gives them a cross-eyed
look, and all of them
suddenly speak to each other—
the most small of them
in its cradle;
on her cot the sister,
on his box the brother:

—But with no tombstone above her,
not a trace,
how in the snows, could one discover
the place?—

Three children, three wretched worms, send a bitter
sob against heaven's high face
and the stars with their golden glitter.

Arn Kurtz

A Father's Lullaby

Through some wild, deserted stretch
the wind is howling like a bitch.
For mother's breast a baby weeps
until in father's arms he sleeps.

Mother ran, but far too slow,
from the fury of the foe.
He took all, and without pity
drove the people from their city.

So the father lulls his babe
with a ballad of the grave.
Other Jews around him shudder,
and the wind's their only cover.

And the tears are in his eyes,
and with him a cold wind cries.
In the forest who'll give heed
to his song, his baby's need?

Still, with sobs he lulls to rest
that poor orphan at his breast,
and his cry takes flame: "Oh please!
A mother here among the trees!"

Sleep, oh sleep, my orphan son.
Don't cry for mother. You have none.
There's no world for such as we—
here is where our bed must be.

Mother used to lull you nightly
with a tune that sparkled brightly.
Father lacks the skill to bring you
such a song as she could sing you.

Mother had the knack of making
gay songs when her heart was breaking;
from the bitterest tunes and times
she invented candy rhymes.

The destroyer took our all:
mother, bread, both roof and wall.
Sleep, my bitter luck! Stop crying!
Life's a ditch for us to lie in.

Sleep, my little orphan; try!
Sleep without a lullaby.
Through the woods her blood ran dry;
I am now your mother . . . I.

Song of a Substitute Mother

Life's gone to ruin and rack—
not one crumb in the sack.
Hush, my child, my curse—
such is our universe.

Typhus grips your mother;
they've shipped your dad away.
In wicked times another
must rock you night and day.

For a Sudeten child
the muddy ground's a bed,
your cradle—thorns gone wild,
your joy—a crust of bread.

Your father's splitting stones
in Hitler's swampy land:
a helpless pack of bones—
deaf and dumb and blind.

Borders sealed too well,
seas horizon-broad—

one dies within a cell,
another on the road.

Dads are digging pits
to hide you from the frost.
In a world like this
love's dug in and lost.

And I—I rock you, boy:
a mother-substitute . . .
May poison-seas destroy
every Hitler-brute!

Life's gone to ruin and rack—
not one crumb in the sack.
Hush, my child, my curse—
such is our universe.

Freidl Trofimov

The Last Lullaby

Lie quiet now, dear child of mine,
and listen to your mother.
She'll sing a sleepsong one last time
and never sing another.

Listen well, my own sweet spirit,
to your mother's song;
from now on you'll never hear it—
not your whole life long.

For the foe is set to harm her,
and a fierce wind's blowing.
At the doorway of a farmer
she'll leave you and keep going.

Child mine, you'll be lulled to slumber
by somebody new.
And you probably will wonder
why she's cradling you.

Hearing her strange tune, you'll ponder—
yearn to understand;
while, a hunted thing, I wander
lonely through the land.

H. Leivick

Little Boy Dreaming

Little boy, dreaming,
my slumbering dear,
into my eyes
you ought not peer.

Bury yourself
as deep as you can
in sleep, oh my darling,
my dreaming young man.

I've died, and through death
I see it plain:
you—my first born—
are the last to remain.

Are you condemned
to be the last one?
Little boy, dreaming,
my own darling son:

If you hear somebody
bitterly cry,
know that it's I
who am weeping, I.

I gather the grasses
of graves, and spread
a mattress that later
will serve as your bed.

When are you coming
to stay with me here,
little boy dreaming,
my slumbering dear?

Avrom Zak

In the Children's Home

Children in little white camp-beds;
walls covered over with toys;
mothers—cold ashes in ovens;
fathers—in deathcamps destroyed.

Children—from villages, churches;
children—from far and from near;
children—from bunkers and ditches;
children—from bloodbaths and fear.

Children—pulled out of the nightmare—
birds that were scattered in storm . . .
Women among the white camp-beds
each in her white uniform:

ready with smiles that are tender,
looks that are loving and bright;
children—like little white angels,
dreaming in camp-beds of white . . .

Tranquil their rosy young faces,
tender young faces in rows,
laugh as they slumber—already
hearing their mothers' hellos;

laugh to their mothers—how sweet the
hands of a mother, how precious!
Children in little white camp-beds;
mothers in ovens—cold ashes.

Chaveh Rosenfarb

Lullaby

Yesterday I perished
and did not give birth to you, child.
My day went down with the shadows;
your morrow's still dumb and blind.

Like a glint in the eye of the sunset
yesterday I went down.
And you, in the dawn, have not yet
unfurled your blossoming crown.

The wind has put out my brightness;
your flame's not yet aglow.
Between yesterday and tomorrow
hardens the hell of now.

There was a splendid story
I studied my whole life long.
I'd have told it to you, my baby,
in hushed, nostalgic song.

That somewhere on distant acres
a peasant ploughs the earth;
from clouds, from the mouths of horses,
a vapor comes steaming forth.

And a gang of young birds circles
above them in the skies.
From sweat that falls on the acres
wheat and joy will rise.

This is what I'd have told you:
a story of blossoms and bread;
but you were not born—the story
of life is death instead.

Neither will your sun rise,
nor did my hope get sown.
In the graveyard of the present
our graves will never be known.

Dora Teitelboim

Shmulik

In the midst of fields and byroads
there's a Home where children stay,
and close by a train goes past
every day at break of day.

Through the shutters, little children
watch the shadows; and they wait,
hopeful that some passenger
will be coming through the gate.

They keep longing for a mother
to arrive and fondle them,
for a father to walk in
and hold them on his knee again.

And they go on dreaming, hoping,
till once more it's time to sleep.
But one Shmulik stays awake;
but one Shmulik guards the street.

Who is it he seeks? who is it
that he sees among the leaves?
whom does he cry out to? whom
does he greet? whom does he grieve?

Every shadow that approaches
looks like mother; one and all
hurry from the railway station
in his mother's long black shawl.

One of eight was little Shmulik;
none remain of all the others.

Winds are wailing lamentations
for his sisters and his brothers.

No more shall his father's singing
wait for him upon the stair.
No more shall his mother come
and run her fingers through his hair.

He could forget that horrid daybreak
on the journey to Lublin
when she hurled him—in a suitcase—
from the boxcar they were in.

He could forgive them and forget them—
all those bitter times—if now
she would stand beside his bed
and bend just once to touch his brow.

But she comes not from Maidanek.
All that comes is one more sun,
probably because it knows
that his mother will not come.

In the midst of fields and roadways
there's a Home where children stay;
and one child—no more than seven—
with a head of hair that's gray.

Moishe Broderson

A New Lullaby

Dolly, dolly, dolly dear,
don't you shed a single tear!
Shut your eyes now, shut them tight.
Dolly, dollykins—good night!

Dolly, dolly, dolly dear,
where now is my mother, where?
Shut your eyes now, shut them tight.
Dolly, dollykins—good night!

Who has killed her, so that she
won't come back to you and me?
Shut your eyes now, shut them tight.
Dolly, dollykins—good night!

Daddy's far away at war,
so we'll see him too no more—
shut your eyes now, shut them tight,
Dolly, dollykins—good night!

All alone they've left me here.
Dolly, dolly—not one tear!
Shut your eyes now, shut them tight.
Dolly, dollykins—good night!

Crying's not the thing to do;
with my dolly I'll sleep too.
Dolly, dollykins—good night!
Let's now lie with eyes shut tight.

In my dream both dad and mom
back to us will surely come.
Shut your eyes now, shut them tight.
Dolly, dollykins—good night!

Avrom Sutzkever

Playthings

Every plaything, my child, hold it precious;
every toy, every frail little form.
And at night, when the flame nods to ashes,
let the stars of the tree keep them warm.

Amid grass that the dew makes delicious,
let him nibble, your pony of gold;
dress your lad up in warm scatter-dashes
when the breath of the seabird blows cold.

Put a panama hat with a feather
on the head of your favorite doll,
because none of your toys has a mother,
and they wail unto God at the wall.

Love them dearly, your little princesses.
I recall such a day—dark and wild—:
seven streets full of porcelain faces
in a city with nary a child.

Shike Driz

Babi-Yar

I'd have picked the right beam for a crib to be swung on,
and have cradled and cradled my Yankel, my young one.
But in fire and flame the hut fell to ashes;
where then am I to rock my boy, my precious?

> To nettles, thorns and thistles
> the village road surrenders;
> the hushed white doves
> have been transformed to cinders.

I'd have chosen a tree; my cradle would have hung there;
I'd have taken my Shloimel, sung him and sung there;
but I've not one thread of his pillow-case,
and of his shoes not so much as a lace.

> Not a twig, not a leaf . . .
> the hearty oak
> is a heap of coals
> that smolder and smoke . . .

I'd have cut off my braids, completely undone them,
and have hung my darlings' cradle upon them;
but I don't know where they are now, the bones—
the priceless bones of my two little sons.

> Help me, mothers, help me
> tear the music from my breast!
> Help me, mothers, help me
> rock Babi-Yar to rest!

The Cradle

The cradle rocks itself
morning and night;
gone from the cradle
is Momma's delight.
Gone from the cradle
is Momma's pleasure;
the cradle rocks itself,
robbed of its treasure.
And goatikin-moatikin,
goatikin gray,
holds one bloody straw
in its mouth today.

David Einhorn

The Empty Little Bed

Lulla, lulla, baby's bed,
baby's bare, deserted bed—
woe unto the mother!
At the foot of baby's bed
lies the little goat, struck dead—
goat and child together.

Lulla, lulla, baby's bed . . .
In my baby's empty bed
lies a knife that glitters . . .
So I rock the steel and moan:
if my belly grew a stone,
it would have been better!

Lulla, lulla, baby's bed . . .
At the foot of baby's bed
wolfish teeth are glaring.
Down they snap—a sound of dread—
from his mouth the blood runs red
and there's none to dare him.

Lulla, lulla, wolf of gray.
Since you've wolfed my child away,
please don't spare its mother.
At the foot of baby's bed
where my little goat lies dead
let us bleed together.

Avrom Sutzkever

The Young Mother

Since there's nothing in the whole wide world, no other
than her baby's doll, what shall she do?
Whom is she to love now, the young mother?
Who shall offer her an answer? Who?

So she shuts the door and double-locks it,
and once more into the bare, bare, bare
cradle she lays down the child and rocks it,
rocks her baby with its porcelain stare.

Every wall and beam is frost-besprinkled—
straw keeps half the wind from coming through.
She puts on a smile, as if she hopes her twinkle
will light up the baby's features too.

But the plaything weeps: her dream's been plundered,
stolen from her outstretched hands somehow.
—Has she, God forbid, got sick, I wonder . . . ?
O, she's burning up! Just feel that brow!

Mother's cooling lips are on her forehead:
Hannele, don't cry! Suppose a wolf
heard you crying—wouldn't that be horrid?
—And she's choking on the tears herself.

And against her breast the mother gently
presses Hannele, and rocks the doll;
and she gives it suck, and murmurs faintly:
Husha, hushabye, my life, my all!

And it sucks. And something foamy bubbles
on its pretty mouth, so pressed to her.
Rocked into a smile are all its troubles;
slightly, as it sleeps, the eyelids stir.

And the mother, clasping her beloved,
also dreams; but with a scream she wakes:
gone the straw—the window's all uncovered,
and, like stars, stream in the wintry flakes.

M. Shenker

Sleep, Child

Sleep, child, sleep;
not in your bed,
but in a heap
of ash, of dead.

You loved to nest
beside your mother.
Do you at least
still lie together?

The furious wind
won't let you slumber;
swift as a fiend
he tears you asunder.

You knew no rest
in your brief career;
and now that it's past,
where are you, where?

To every flurry
of wind I say:
"Did you not carry
my child away?"

I ask the earth,
I ask the sky:
"Have you not heard
my baby's cry?"

Could I have kept
at least your mother,
we might have wept
for you together.

Moishe Shulshtein

Cradlesong 1943

I'll sing a lullaby to you, my dear,
such as has never yet been heard or sung
since the first lullaby was sung somewhere
and since the day the world's first cradle swung.
I am your cradle, you whose embers died
before you were ignited, and before
you knew my rocking hand; now deep inside
I lull you into sleep forevermore.

Your first cry, as you left your mother's womb,
was certain to have been a horror-roar.
Chains would have been the leggings you first wore.
Live-wire would be the first heat you'd have known,
and your first covering would have been shame;
so I have wrapped your body in my own
and sent you off to the far land of dream.

If the first word to you be snarled by brutes,
if your first footstep be on homeless ways,
and day and night one of the cutthroat troops
stood guard above you with his cruel face,
rather than let his grip destroy you, child,
I keep you hidden safe inside of me,
and the extinguished smile you never smiled
will glimmer through my skin transparently.

I've often seen your cradle flaming, all
the earth ablaze, and every plant on fire:
in trees the nests burn—with the swallow's call
and the whole twittering of April's choir.
My head is also ravaged by the flames;
into my hair the conflagration climbs.
Sleep, so that not a single ash remains
of you: memento of these burning times.

With icy prongs of steel in the hot flesh
your burning joy snuffs out my own bright blood.
But fury kindles it to flame afresh
until I reach that blessed interlude
when song no more will cradle you to die
and life will be condemned as sin no more;
but now take from me my last lullaby—
be wafted, child, to dreamland's distant shore.

> Sleep, my wonder that did not unfold;
> sleep, my joyous calm not granted me;
> sleep, my pride I'm never to behold;
> sleep, life of my life that will not be.

Simche Sneh

A Song Without a Name
about a Child Without a Name

A tree on the roadside leans,
leans as if it's crying.
Close by, where the grass is green,
a glaze-eyed child is lying.

He was called . . . well, what did they call him?
Does it matter what name he had then?
What matters is that he's fallen
and won't call out again.

He lies in the grass, not far
from the golden rows of grain;
and on his throat the scar
of a spiked boot remains.

And there's one more crimson spot
in the middle of his head—
just like a quivering shot,
just like a pearl of red.

But—pearls are white . . . All the same,
does it matter? What matters instead
is—he was called by a name;
he called—and now lies dead—

Itzik Manger

Orphans

The peacock's gold and the pure white goat
rock cradles robbed of their young;
since sainted Yankele is no more,
no lullaby needs to be sung.

The gold of the peacock is lonely gold;
and the goat, that faun of grace—
dazzling as sorrowful snow—these are
the orphans of my race.

Noteh's Sleep-Song

I sing myself a sleep-song:
"Sleep, sleep, you lonesome man.
It was your fate to be buried
in far Uzbekistan."

The wind rocks your grave softly:
"Sleep, Noteh, sleep, liu-liu.
When eyes are shut, the stillness
grows brighter, purer for you.

"Hear the song of the wildgrass,
of the wildflowers in the field;
don't rage that earth is above you
and that the stars are concealed.

"The stars, those silver bastards,
have tricked both the dead and alive—
millions who've piously waited
for Messiah to arrive.

"Hear the sparrow-hawks cawing
as over the earth they wheel
with beaks so sharp and bloody,
they're welcome to any meal!

"So thank the earth that hides you
in her loyal, deep embrace.
She's raised a rose and a sunflower
to mark your resting-place.

"This monument will blossom
and wither and blossom anew—
October will blow out its fire,
and May will relight it for you.

"And possibly your brother
will happen to wander by
and grace your grave with your vision—
a song that will not die.

"Meanwhile it's the clouds that wander
in their old, eternal way—
figures, plants, chimeras
from now till Judgment Day."

I sing myself a sleep-song:
"Sleep, sleep, you lonesome man.
It was your fate to be buried
in far Uzbekistan."

Menachem Boraishe

Over Cradles

Over the cradles at slumbertime
mothers rock their babies with rhyme,
sweet rhymes of raisins and almonds.
Mothers—breasts of dried-up sacks;
children—heads on toothpick necks.
And hoarsely Death hums along
over the cradles the sweet song
of raisins and of almonds.

In cellars, in caves deep underground
not yet found by the murderous hound,
amid tomorrow's holy slain
short-lived matings flash into flame.

Fingers entwine and the generations
that will never be born raise lamentations;
the generations that will never arrive
flood these young loins with their lust to be alive;
and the blaze, the blood of the never-to-be
burst forth in this one brief ecstasy.

What is One?
One is the mother's refrain
lulling her children before death;
One—the bloodsong in the veins,
eternity in the minutes before death.

H. Leivick

Under the Patch of Yellow

Under the patch of yellow
shut your eyelids tight.
Sleep, my little fellow.
Your father's in Dachau tonight.

Where is Dachau, and what is
father doing there?
He's a good Jew, and that is
what you must be, my dear.

To the whip, to the bars, to the snarling
there drops a bloodied head.
Your forehead's on fire, darling!
Hush, it was not your dad.

I'll scare you no more, my precious,
with tales of the tortured and bound.
Sometimes they are square, the patches,
and sometimes they are round.

Sometimes a patch is crimson,
but yellow is used much more.
Your father—dream about him, son;
dream that he stands at the door.

He turns the key to our hovel
and steps inside with a smile.
A father has no trouble
finding the bed of his child.

He rocks asleep your crying,
and rocks himself as well;
lies down, and remains lying—
no need for Dachau's hell.

Your father is everlasting,
as everlasting rest,
as is our yellow patching.
Hush now, sleep is best.

Meyer-Zimmel Tkatch

Cradlesong of a Jewish Mother in Poland

Husha-hush, my little Jew,
branch of a great line.
Here's a lullaby that's new,
though in olden rhyme.

Tell me—where's your cradle, child?
Gone—without a trace.
Gone the little goat; a wild
beast is in its place.

Scorpions and vipers nest
in your ravaged home;
in this hole tonight we'll rest;
here we'll hide unknown.

Keen as wolf-eyes, searching fires
flicker all around,
on the prowl for Itche-Mayers
I'll keep watch; sleep sound!

Little goats and little lambs,
little Jews—God's sheep—
fall like flies inside the camps.
Sleep, fugitive, sleep!

You shall be their Kaddish, you—
clear-voiced Jacob's son!
You shall lift their cry anew:
Our Lord God is One! . . .

Husha-hush, my little Jew;
wracked with grief am I,
that I should be singing you
such a lullaby.

Jacob Glatstein

Ghetto Song

Within your bones my singing
melts like the snow's first flakes.
Within your starry eyes
an old joy reawakes.
Laugh, my darling child!
Sing, my grief, my prize!
Over an old wall
seven suns arise.

From the boughs and branches
a weary Sabbath weeps.
Beggarfolk sit dead
on all the gloomy streets.
Hush, my darling child!
Sleep, my tender flesh!
On your shiny platter
dances a golden fish.

Where your father passes,
the stars bestow their grace.
The moon's his dear possession
through the nightly chase.
Sleep, my darling child!
Kisses shut your eyes!
Over grieving ruins
a young dove flies.

The dove is you, of course;
your hands are its white wings.
Beside your hungry cradle
Mother sits and sings.
Shush, my darling child!
Just you hush and wait!
The good hands of your father
are opening the gate.

Itzik Feffer

Cradlesong

Do not sleep, my darling child;
now's no time for dreams.
Hear the flame: it hammers wild
at the roof, and screams.

Now's no time for me to sing;
hush, soul, weep no more.
Hear the storm with bow and string
play his waltz of war.

No, my love, no time to sleep—
not while thunders boom, not while
shadows mutely weep
in your little room . . .

Through your pane a swarm of stars
sightlessly are gaping.
In this pretty bed of yours
night now lies a-sleeping.

See, my child, how yesterday's
happy phantom flutters.
Like a star your father's face
sparkles through the shutters.

He lies camped with shell and wire
in a snow-heaped land,
and he sends the foe his fire
with his mighty hand.

And his call across the snow
rouses all who hear it.
When you're grown, my darling, show
you've your father's spirit!

Shmerke Katcherginsky

Softly, Softly

Softly, softly! let's be silent:
graves are growing here.
They were sown by our tormentors;
green they grow, and fair.
Toward Panar run roads aplenty;
from Panar not one;
father's disappeared, and with him
all our joy is gone.
Quiet, child! don't cry, my treasure;
weeping is in vain.
Those who hate us will not ever
understand our pain.
There are shores around the seas;
prisons, too, have boundaries;
but for all our grief
there's no relief,
no relief.

Spring, that gifts the land with showers,
gives us autumn's loss.
Though the days now swarm with flowers,
only night sees us.
In the gold of autumn's weather
bloom our wildest woes:
the child's torn from his orphaned mother;
to Panar he goes.
Like the frozen Vilya River
yoked in agony,
Lithuania delivers
ice-floes to the sea.
Somewhere all this gloom is breaking,
from the darkness suns awaken.
Horseman, full speed!
Your child—hear him plead,
hear him plead.

Softly, softly, wells are bubbling
deep within the heart.
Till the hell-gate comes a-tumbling,
our lips must never part.
Don't be merry, child; your twinkle
would betray us now.
Let our foe see spring unwrinkle
—a leaf on autumn's bough!
Let the well keep calmly running;
keep your hope unheard—
with freedom, father will be coming—
sleep, my love, my bird.
Like the Vilya, freely streaming,
like the trees reborn and greening,
freedom's light will blaze
upon your face,
upon your face.

Brache Kopstein

War Lullaby

Sleep, my child, my only child,
rest, my one delight!
Across the world a wind that's wild
is blowing out the light.

Down all the highroads, dazed and scattered,
victims drag themselves along;
the earth's best things lie crushed and shattered
and the word dies on my tongue.

Sleep, my child, my only child,
rest, my one delight!
I want to sing, my son, my pride,
of how one day you'll fight.

When you're a man—all heart and muscle—
you'll laugh, recalling what I said.
Meanwhile, darling, bullets whistle,
cannons boom around your head.

Sleep, my child, my only child,
rest, my one delight!
It's I who guard your life meanwhile
with mine, both day and night.

May you become a man of power
and face the foe in mortal war.
Your day, that follows this dark hour,
will burst in brightness at your door.

Chanan Kiel

Partisans

Huts still huddle sleeping;
the field-dogs bark in chorus.
Rag-bag Jews are escaping
into the deeps of the forest.

Hushed as grass, from the ghetto
the Jews went, holding their breath—
in Polish glade and meadow
they'll be partisans—to the death!

To live till the war is done
amid the wilds of the wood,
emerging, each with a gun,
to pay for blood with blood;

to settle accounts, we'll find them,
destroy their peaceful slumber,
and for each crime remind them
there are Jews with guns who remember.

Huts still huddle sleeping;
the field-dogs bark in chorus.
Jews with grenades are creeping
out of the deeps of the forest.

Leizer Wolf

Cradlesong

Sleep, my child;
the night is dropping
on each valley,
on each hill now.
Everywhere
the wheels are stopping.
No more grain
from any mill now.

> For the Germans,
> for the Germans,
> may you, millwheels,
> turn no longer.
> May their bellies
> swell with hunger,
> swell with hunger.

Long ago
the sun went under.
All the stars
have started gleaming,
and the stalks
are sunk in slumber
to their knees
in moonlight dreaming.

> For the Germans,
> for the Germans,
> may you, stalks,
> not turn to wheat.
> May they fall from hunger,
> may they soon
> stretch out their feet.

Who's that knocking
at this hour?
Darling dove,
don't shake so much.
When he's in
your father's power,
he'll get more
than just a touch.

Hush, child; in
he swaggers, bringing
ready bayonet
and snort:
"From a tree
you'll soon be swinging
if your husband
won't report."

Hush, child.
For our sake your father
will do wonders—
no more weeping!
Now we two
will rock together,
on a different
gallows sleeping.

For the Germans,
for the Germans,
may you, stalks,
not turn to wheat.
May they fall from hunger,
stretch their feet out
at our feet.

Adela Friedman

A Wind Weeps

Forgive me, dear child,
that I won't lull you
with those charming tales
I used to tell you.
Somewhere there's a wind; it cries,
demands of us, reminds us
that now we need new lullabies.

Hush, my darling, go to sleep.
Whom now does the wind beweep?
Beyond the hill that's turning green
the wind today is sorrowing
for mother's only child and care,
lives that were tender, young and dear.

And it moans, and moan by moan
pushes into every home,
and if in one a Jew should dwell,
he lights a candle now, in honor
of the warrior who fell
in the ravaged ghetto hell
lifting high his freedom-banner!

Dearest boy, don't cry, don't cry.
The ghetto-hero chose to die
so that all ghettos would be gone!
Forgive, forgive your mother, son,
that it is not of goats I sing.
Like a link within a ring
on this day with everyone
the noble ghetto-song I sing:

Now, on the day of days, "To your last breath
don't say you're on the road to death!"

The Poets

Menachem Boraishe (1888–1949). *Born in 1888, Menachem Boraishe (originally Goldberg) studied with his father, a Brest-Litovsk Hebrew teacher, then in a Russian city-school. A Poale-Zionist at sixteen, he wrote verse in Russian and Yiddish. Taking his work to Warsaw in 1905, he was praised and published by I. L. Peretz. From 1909 to 1911, he served in the Russian army. Three years later he attacked the anti-Semitic boycott with a bitter poem, "Poland," and at the outset of the war left for Switzerland, then settled in New York. In 1916, with M. L. Halpern,* he edited the anthology East Broadway. *That year his first collection,* Chained, *also appeared. A mammoth poem,* Sand, *followed four years later. Even more ambitious was the narrative* Knight Saul, *issued in Warsaw in 1923. A biblical drama,* The Shepherd David, *was published in Vilna in 1932. From 1933 to 1947 he worked for the American Jewish Congress and helped edit its* Congress Weekly. *He died in New York early in 1949.*

Moishe Broderson (1890–1956). *Born in Moscow in 1890, Moishe Broderson was brought up by an uncle in a Byelorussian town, then joined his father, who had settled earlier in Lodz. His first collection,* Black Leaves, *appeared in 1913. Through World War I and the revolution he lived in Moscow, then returned to Lodz for twenty years. There he authored such volumes as* Pearls in the Trough *(1920) and other children's books. In 1939, he fled east before the Nazi invasion. The same year,* Fifty Poems *appeared. He became involved in experimental theater, and his play* Before the Holiday *was performed in Moscow in 1947. Unlike many of his colleagues, he survived the murders of 1952. He was banished to a Siberian slave-labor camp, from which he was freed in 1955. A year after his release he died in Warsaw. His* Selected Writings *were issued in Buenos Aires in 1959. In 1970, he was reinterred in Haifa. Four years later* The Last Song *was published in Tel Aviv.*

Shike Driz (1908–71). *Shike Driz was born in Krasna, the Ukraine, in 1908. He was widely known for his children's poems; his* Bright Reality *appeared in 1930 and* Steel Might *in 1934. A Red Army volunteer, he served in Galician border towns from 1939 to 1941, aiding many refu-*

gees from the Nazis as well as local Jewish villagers. Afterward, he lived in Moscow. His final collection, The Fourth Rail, *appeared two years before his death in 1971.*

David Einhorn (1886–1973). *David Einhorn was born in 1886 in Karelitch, Novgorod (then Russia), the son of an army doctor. At thirteen, he began writing in Hebrew, but the revolutionary tide drew him close to the Bund and he turned to Yiddish, publishing first in Vilna's Bundist press, then in journals worldwide. His first collection,* Quiet Songs, *appeared in Vilna in 1909, as did his second book,* My Songs, *three years later. Jailed for his radical associations the same year, he was expelled from Russia and emigrated first to France, then to Switzerland. In 1917,* To a Jewish Daughter *was issued. After World War I, he settled first in Warsaw, then in Berlin, where his* Requiem, *memorializing the war's ten million casualties, was published in 1922, and his* Collected Poems *three years later. By then he had moved to Paris, which he fled before the Nazi onslaught. He arrived in New York in 1940, where his poems of the Holocaust appeared in 1943, followed by* Collected Poems 1904–1951 *in 1952. He died on March 2, 1973.*

Bezalel Friedman (1897–1941). *Bezalel Friedman was born in Brest-Litovsk in 1897, the son of a cigarette-worker. At nineteen, he became a Poale-Zionist and taught in a Sokolov school for young war victims. His first poems were published in 1919. The following year, with his wife, Bertha Lellchuk, a future actress, he moved to Palestine. In 1922, disillusioned with Zionism, they left for New York with their infant daughter. He became a Workmen's Circle teacher in 1924, and three years later helped found the Union Square Writers Union, which published his first collection,* Illuminated Roads, *in 1929. Through the 1930s he was an outstanding teacher, whose students still meet annually to honor him. In 1936, the Proletpen's* Signal *issued his second volume,* The Forgotten Person, *a remarkable novel in verse. He died five years later, as the Holocaust exploded eastward.*

Jacob Glatstein (see p. 210).

Shmerke Katcherginsky (see p. 121).

Benjamin Katz (1905–   ). *Born in Horodnitza, the Ukraine, in 1905, Benjamin Katz left for Canada at fifteen and remained there until*

1937. A printer by trade, he also taught Yiddish in the Workmen's Circle schools of Windsor, Boston, Detroit, and New York. His poems, proletarian in nature, began appearing in 1924, and he contributed to the Proletpen's journals, Hammer *and* Signal, *as well as to the* Morning Freiheit. *Among his collections of poetry are* Dawn *(1928, with others),* Spetzaine *(1930), and* The Dream of Brothers, *(1947). With his wife, the poet Brache Kopstein, he settled in Tel Aviv in 1949. There, in 1976, they edited an anthology of Yiddish lullabies,* Under Yankele's Cradle.

Chanan Kiel (1910–   ). *Chanan Kiel (shortened from Kieltziglovsky) was born in Tchenstochov in 1910. He graduated from the Hebrew high school and teachers' seminary. He fled east before the Nazis, but left the Soviet Union after the war, as did many other émigré poets, and settled in New York in 1947. Here he contributed poems to* Tsukunft *and other periodicals. His books are* In All Colors *(1971), and* A Shepherd in an Alien Land *(1979).*

Kehos Kliger (1904–1985). *Son of a composer and cantor. Kehos Kliger was born in Vladimir-Volinsky (Ludmir) in 1904. He attended a ye-shiva, then studied in Yiddish and Polish public schools. At twenty, he began contributing poetry to local journals and was soon being published in Warsaw. Political persecution drove him into exile in Argentina in 1936. Beginning in 1941 with* Singing on the Earth, *he produced an impressive series of collections culminating with* The Barefoot Week: Songs and Ballads 1937–1957, I and the Sea *(1958),* The Lovely Rose *(1964), and* Harp and Hammer *(1976). He translated from Spanish, Polish, Hebrew, and English (including a volume of Whitman's poems and Odets's play* Awake and Sing!). *He died in Buenos Aires on April 20, 1985.*

Brache Kopstein (1909–   ). *Born in Priluki, near Kiev, in 1908, Brache Kopstein lived with her grandfather in Kishinev after being orphaned at eleven. Migrating to Winnipeg, Canada, in 1924, she worked by day and went to night school. She moved to New York in 1933. Her poetry began appearing two years later in* Literary Leaves *(Warsaw). Her collections include* I Am Strong *(1939),* Sing My Heart *(1945),* The People Are Here *(1951), and* Selected Poems *(1968). With her husband, Benjamin Katz, she settled in Tel Aviv in 1949. Her brother was the distinguished Soviet choral director Moishe Kopstein.*

Arn Kurtz (1891–1964). *Arn Kurtz was born in 1891 in Asve, near Vitebsk, Byelorussia. At thirteen, he began wandering through the big cities of Russia, working in theaters and circuses as a barber, his lifelong trade. At eighteen he returned to his father's home in the village of Old-Sloboda. Two years later, he migrated to Philadelphia, where his first poems, under the pseudonym "Azrael," appeared in 1916 in* Jewish World *and in Z. Weinper's* At the First *four years later. He also published several journals of his own before moving to New York, where his work appeared in* In Zick. *His first collection,* Chaos, *appeared in Philadelphia in 1920. By 1926 he had joined the Communist Party and from then on he contributed exclusively to left-wing publications:* Morning Freiheit, Hammer, Signal, Zamlungen, Yiddishe Kultur, Sovietish Heimland. *Among his works are* Placards *(1927),* The City of Gold *(1935),* No Pasaran *(1938), and* Marc Chagall *(1946). From 1957 until his death seven years later, he published his own quarterly,* Poems of Today. *His selected poems, utterly omitting his pre-Communist work, were seen through the press in 1966 by his widow, the poet Olga Cabral.*

Zische Landau (1889–1937). *Born in 1889 in Plotzk, Poland, of a famous rabbinical family, Zische Landau was orphaned early and emigrated to the United States in 1906. Here he worked as a house painter. The year he arrived, his first poem was printed in the* Jewish Daily Forward. *Five years later, he was among the leaders of Di Yunge. He died early in 1937 in New York. His collected comedies,* Nothing Happened, *and a collected edition of his poems in three volumes appeared later that year. A decade passed before his brilliant translations from world poetry were published in book form.*

Itzik Manger (see p. 229).

Kadia Molodowsky (see p. 208).

Mani-Leib (1883–1953). *Mani-Leib, whose family name was Brahinsky, was born in 1883 in the Ukrainian village of Nyezhin. His father was a peddler, his mother sold vegetables, and he himself became a shoemaker. Active in the revolutionary movement, he left Russia for London in 1904 and published his first poems there. A year later, he settled in New York, where he led the aestheticist rebellion of 1907 and was published in its journal* Shriftn. *In 1918,* Poems, Jewish and Slavic Motifs, Ballads, *and* The Song of Bread *were published.* Clever Little-Tongued Lad *and*

Little Flower–Little Garlands *followed four years later. In 1930,* Miracle after Miracle *was published, and his children's biography of Mendele Moicher Sforim appeared in 1936. He died in New York in 1953. Two years later his widow, Rachel Veprinski, prepared his two-volume* Songs and Ballads *for publication, and in 1961, his* Sonnets *appeared in Paris.*

Melech Ravitch (1893–1976). *Melech Ravitch was born Zachariah Berger in 1893 in Radimno, Eastern Galicia. His early volumes include* At the Threshold *and* Spinoza *(1918). He lived in Vienna after World War I; then, along with Peretz Markish, he led Warsaw's rambunctious "gang" of Khaliastre poets in the mid-1920s. Among his books of that time are* The Kernel of My Songs *and* Prehistoric Landscapes, *both published in 1922, and* Blood on the Flag, *issued in 1929. Later he became a world traveler—his* Continents and Oceans *was published in 1937—and in 1941 he settled in Canada.* The Songs of My Songs, *a selected edition, appeared in 1954. The same year, he moved to Israel but in 1958 returned to Montreal, where he completed an ambitious biographical encyclopedia of Yiddish writers and a major autobiography,* The Story of My Life. *He died in Montreal in 1976.*

Chaveh Rosenfarb (1923–   ). *Chaveh Rosenfarb was born in Lodz in 1923. Soon after graduating from its Polish-Jewish high school, she was among the thousands incarcerated in the ghetto of Lodz. While there, she wrote many poems and parts of a novel,* Three Trees of Life. *She survived Auschwitz and Bergen-Belsen. After the war she taught in a Brussels Yiddish school. Her* Ballad of Yesterday's Forest *appeared in London in 1947. A year later, her* Song of the Jewish Waiter Abram *was issued there first, then—with the addition of ghetto poems and fragments of a diary—in Montreal, where she settled in 1950 and completed her studies at the Yiddish Teachers' Seminary. In 1958, her drama of the Vilna ghetto,* The Bird of the Ghetto, *was published in Montreal and performed in Israel by the Habimah. Her completed ghetto novel was issued in Tel Aviv in 1972. Seven years later, she received the prestigious Itzik Manger Award.*

Moishe Shulshtein (1911–81). *Moishe Shulshtein was born in Koriv, Poland in 1911. He studied in Hebrew and Yiddish schools. Moving to Warsaw with his parents in 1923, he learned the tailor's trade and attended evening school. His first poems were published in the journal* Our Hope, *and he was included in the 1936 Minsk anthology* Life and

Struggle. *At first a Poale-Zionist, he later became a Communist. In 1937, he moved to Paris, but went into hiding in various towns after the Nazi occupation. He joined the Resistance, and for a time was impris-oned by the Gestapo. After the war, his work appeared in many publica-tions, and in Kadia Molodowsky's* Poems of the Holocaust. *Along with Binem Heller and other poets, he turned away from the Left toward the end of the 1950s and embraced a more national ideology. He died in 1981.*

Isaiah Spiegel (1906–90). *Born in Lodz in 1906, Isaiah Spiegel at-tended Hebrew and Yiddish schools as a boy, then trained at a teachers' college. For a decade, he taught Yiddish and Jewish literature. With the arrival of the Nazi troops, he was among the many thousands penned in the ghetto of Lodz. There he wrote and buried a large number of ghetto stories. Although he survived Auschwitz, the rest of his family was wiped out. After the war he recovered his manuscripts and published them in three priceless volumes. He resumed his teaching career, but left Poland for Israel in 1951. Until his death in 1990 he steadily produced essays, fiction, and poetry of high quality.*

Avrom Sutzkever (see p. 125).

Dora Teitelboim (see p. 242).

Meyer-Zimmel Tkatch (1894–1986). *Meyer-Zimmel Tkatch was born in 1894 in Priborsk, a Ukrainian village near Kiev. At nineteen he emigrated to the United States, where he became a house painter. His first poems, in Russian, were published in 1914. Afterward he turned to Yiddish, and his work—fables as well as poems—appeared in many journals, including those of the Left. He first collection,* At God's Behest *(1927), was followed by several more in the 1930s, all published in Chi-cago. A volume of Holocaust poems,* Blood Shrieks from the Ground, *was issued in 1946. Then came* From Generation to Generation *(1947),* Thirst for the Source *(1952),* Fall of Leaves *(1960), and* Mein Hob un Gob *(My Treasures and My Gifts), a 1962 two-volume collected edition. These were followed by* Fruits of Age from the Blossoms of Youth *(1971),* My Anthology of Russian Poetry *(1973), and* One's Own and Another's *(1977). His home was New York, and it was there that he died in 1986.*

Freidl Trofimov. *Freidl Trofimov, a longtime resident of Los Angeles, was born in the early 1900s. She evokes her poor childhood in "My Village Lahishn" and her Chicago years in "Chicago in the Spring." "Not to Forget, Not to Forgive" memorializes the Holocaust, including a memorable scene in which Hirsh Glik's "Partisan Song" is triumphantly sung on the streets of Jerusalem.*

Leizer Wolf (1910–1943). *Born in 1910, Leizer Wolf was among the young Vilna poets, along with Chaim Grade and Avrom Sutzkever, galvanized by the genius of Moishe Kulbak, then a Vilna teacher. In 1931, he met the eighteen-year-old Sutzkever, whose home district of Shnipikov soon became the center of an exciting new group, Young Vilna. Under his leadership a dazzling cluster of newcomers published in its journal,* Young Vilna. *It was Wolf who encouraged the child-poet of Shnipikov, Hirsh Glik, to turn from Hebrew to Yiddish and to organize a junior group paralleling Young Vilna. Under Wolf's guidance they issued a journal named for their group,* Young Forest. *When the Nazis took Vilna he succeeded where Sutzkever failed: he escaped to the Soviet Union. There, in the grip of Samarkand's cold and hunger, he perished in 1943. Only a small part of his huge output has survived.*

Avrom Zak (see p. 167).

Poets of the Holocaust

Songs of the Ghettos and Death Camps

Although Terezin was unique, other ghettos and death camps produced lyrics and music. Their quality as verse may not be of the highest, but some are stirring when sung, and as human documents they are remarkable. Included here are songs and poems created in or near Bialystok, Bremen, Cracow, Kovno, Lodz, Petivia (France), Shavel, Vilna, Vittel (France), Warsaw, and an unknown shtetl in Galicia.

Thanks to Shmerke Katcherginsky, whose lovingly edited anthology of Holocaust songs has been among my chief sources, we know in some cases the circumstances of their creation, who many of their composers were, in what theatrical revues they were introduced to the doomed inmates, and—often—the fate of their creators. Whatever facts are known will accompany the texts.

Several of these poets had published seriously prior to their incarceration. In their cases, biographical paragraphs will be given. One cannot begin to conjecture how many of their works did not miraculously survive. Perhaps the finest of the walled-in poets was Miriam Ulinover, born in 1890. According to a survivor, she wrote prolifically in the Lodz ghetto, but not a trace of her Holocaust poetry has remained; perhaps it came with her to Auschwitz, in whose crematorium she perished in August 1944.

Authors Unknown

In Bialystok's Ghetto

In Bialystok's gray ghetto, a cry of anguish wakes—
in Bialystok's gray ghetto, the heart within us breaks.

> We sit and wonder, some of us:
> What is to become of us?
> They drive us, yellow patch on the lapel,
> along the street like souls in Hell.

> Women drag their children
> into the Judenrat
> and ask about their husbands:
> "How long before they're back?"

Let Us Be Jolly

Let us be jolly and share good jokes:
we'll yet sit shiveh when Hitler croaks.

> Biri-bi, bam-bam-bam,
> biri-bi, bam-bam-bam.

Let us take comfort, forget our sorrow;
through Hitler's body the worms will burrow.

> Biri-bi, bam . . .

Who drive us now to Treblinka's horror
themselves will be under the ground tomorrow.

> Biri-bi, bam . . .

Arm in arm, we'll yet make merry
and dance through a German cemetery.

Biri-bi, bam-bam-bam,
biri-bi, bam-bam-bam.

(Warsaw Ghetto)

Not One Sob

Nations, let there be no crying—
mother, child, gone from the nest?
Such are the days now, days of dying—
an evil wind blows from the west.

    Not one sob, no tears be shed:
    hard as steel, and hearts of stone.
    There'll be better times ahead,
    good as any times we've known.

Don't weep, dear friend, don't moan in sorrow
that life is just a lottery:
today I may be yours, tomorrow
perhaps the wheel will stop for me.

    Not one sob, no tears be shed:
    hard as steel, and hearts of stone.
    There'll be better times ahead,
    good as any times we've known.

(Kovno Ghetto)

From Vilna Went Forth Still Another Decree

From Vilna went forth still another decree:
to fetch in the village Jews quickly.
So all were assembled, the young and the old,
with litters to carry the sickly.

The gates of the camp were then bolted,
and each of the newcomers sorted:

the people from Ushmen remained, and to Kovno
the Sulites must now be transported.

So out of the camp the young victims
were ushered one after the other,
and into the cars they were thrust with dispatch—
like cattle, were sealed in together.

The train chugged along without hurry;
it hooted; the sirens kept screeching.
At a station called Pogar it ground to a halt,
and next came the sound of unhitching . . .

They saw in an instant: they'd all been deceived,
it was to their death they'd been taken!
They broke down the doors of the boxcars, and tried
to snatch at some way of escaping.

They hurled themselves fiercely against the Gestapo,
and tore the brown shirt from his body
Not far from the martyred, there also lay dead
some storm troopers, bitten and bloody.

David Beigelman
(1884–1944)

Born in Lodz in 1884 to a family of musicians, David Beigelman at-tended a cheder and a Russian public school. From an early age he composed for and played in the orchestras of Poland's Yiddish theaters. Later he arranged hundreds of Yiddish folksongs and composed settings for the texts of various Yiddish poets. He lived in Lodz until 1939, then in its ghetto, where he served as music director of a small Yiddish theater, wrote essays on music for the People's Press, *and composed songs. In August 1944, at the liquidation of the Lodz ghetto, he was shipped to Auschwitz, where he perished.*

Gypsy Song
(excerpt)

The night is dark,
as dark as ink.
With quaking heart
I think and think.
No others live in
such grief as we're given
We go unfed:
no crust of bread.

(Lodz Ghetto)

Kasriel Broida
(1907–1945)

Kasriel Broida was born in Vilna (1907), graduated from the Hebrew secondary school, and became involved in Yiddish theater—in various troupes as well as amateur circles and the marionette-theater Meidim. He himself wrote theater pieces that proved enormously popular. After the Nazi occupation, he not only organized several revue programs for those trapped with him in the Vilna ghetto—including Years of Corn and Days of Wheat *and* One Can't Know Anything—*but also composed songs that were performed in almost all the ghettos and death camps (*"Ghetto, I'll Never Forget You," "Narrow, Our Room Is Narrow," "Women, Born in Difficult Hours," *and* "I'm Among the Transported"*). As he prepared to stage* Moses Stands Firm, *the Gestapo transported him to the death camps of Estonia and, in January 1945, murdered him.*

Toward a Better Tomorrow

In gray, hard times, when winds are fierce,
when storms control the universe,
there is no use in shedding tears,
in crying. "Such must be our curse."
It's a wind that rips whole limbs asunder.
It's a wind that howls through every bone.
We merely bend; we've not gone under:
we'll straighten, and go striding on!

We'll stride toward a better tomorrow,
go on to a sunnier day;
though joy may be hidden by sorrow,
before us still blazes the way.
Far off it is gleaming—
the world of our dreaming:
all magic, all flowers, all free;
that magical weaving

is what we believe in;
we know for a fact: it will be!

(Vilna Ghetto)

Mordecai Gebirtig
(1877–1942)

Mordecai Gebirtig, whose family name was Bertig, was born in 1877 in Cracow and worked there all his life as a carpenter. Encouraged by Abraham Reisen in 1906, he became a prolific and immensely popular songwriter, composing the melodies as well as the lyrics. From 1914 until the end of World War I, he served in the Austrian army. Two years later, his first collection, Folkstimlich *(In the Popular Tradition) was published. In 1936* My Songs, *fifty of his poems and musical settings, appeared. When a pogrom shattered Pzytyk in 1938, he responded with "Aflame!" This song, prophetic of the Holocaust about to befall them, swept the Jewish communities of Eastern Europe and is still widely known. When Hitler occupied Cracow, Gebirtig was put into the ghetto with his fellow townsmen and was among those shot to death on June 4, 1942. Four years later his collection,* Aflame!, *was published in Cracow. A month before his death he wrote a furiously ironic song, "It's Good," reminiscent of the more famous earlier verses. Here is the opening stanza:*

It's good, it's good, it's good.
The little Jews cry: It's good.
The foe, the ferocious,
moves frightful and swift;
wherever he comes
utter ruin is left,
and little Jews cry: It's good.
And little Jews smile—it's good.
It's fine, just see!
As fine as can be.

Aflame!

Aflame! Brothers! aflame!
There may come the moment of shame
when the town and you expire
together in ashes and fire.
Aside from its black, bare walls

not one trace will remain.
And you stand and look around
with hands that are tame.
And you stand and look around
while our town goes up in flame.

Aflame! Brothers! aflame!
Yours will be the praise or the blame.
If you've loved this town all your days,
take buckets and put out the blaze.
With your own blood put it out.
Show from what stock you came.
Don't stand, brothers, like this
with hands that are tame!
Don't stand and look around
while our town goes up in flame.

Aflame! Brothers! aflame!
Alas, our poor town is aflame.
The more these tongues of fire
consume, the more they desire.
And the wicked winds are droning—
everything's aflame.
Don't stand, brothers, like this
with hands that are tame!
Brothers, don't stand and look around
while our town goes up in flame.

Chaneh Haitin

(1925–   )

*Born in Shavel (Shawly), Lithuania, in 1925, Chaneh Haitin attended
a Hebrew high school, after which she worked in the brush factory in the
ghetto of Shawly. From there she was moved to several German concentra-
tion camps. After liberation, she went first to Lodz, then through Ger-
many and on to Israel, where she settled. Her songs, especially the one that
follows, had been immensely popular in the ghettos and death camps;
some are still sung. From 1945 to 1949 her poems continued to appear,
first in Lodz, then in various Yiddish publications in Germany. In Israel,
S. Meltzer translated her poems into Hebrew. One of her songs, with
music by David Beigelman, depicts in almost cinematic detail the squalor
of the Shawly ghetto—which, due to its extreme hilliness, had been nick-
named The Caucasus:*

> . . . Every puddle is a lake,
> each house in a sorry state.
> Every dwelling's like a stall—
> take a footstep, and you fall.
> Turn a doorknob anywhere,
> swarms of hands and feet are there.
> So is each house hereabout;
> one sees nobody come out . . .

A Jewish Child

In a Lithuanian town
there's a house that stands alone.
Through a narrow window glass
children watch the seasons pass:
little boys with clever heads,
little girls with long blond braids,
and, amid the rest, a pair
of black eyes keeps vigil there.

Charming eyes as black as coal,
and a nose that's cute and small,

lips—created to be kissed—
black curls no one could resist.
Mother brought him wrapped from sight
in the middle of the night,
sobbed, and with a kiss half-wild,
this she whispered to her child:

—Here, my child, your place will be.
Listen carefully to me.
I will leave you here because
Danger's opening its jaws.
With these children nicely play,
just be quiet, and obey.
Not one Jewish word from you;
you no longer are a Jew.

Bitterly he pleads with her:
"Can't we stay the way we were?
Please don't leave me here alone."
And his tears come rolling down.
She bestows kiss after kiss,
but he's not assuaged by this;
still he argues: "No!" and "No!
I won't stay and let you go!"

So she lifts him in her arms;
with a voice that lulls and charms,
"Oh my son," she sings to him,
and he slips into a dream.
Now her grief flows unconfined;
and she leaves the house behind
full of worry, full of fright,
and retreats into the night.

Cold outdoors, a wind blows wild,
and a voice cries, "Oh my child,
to strange hands I've trusted you;
there was nothing else to do."
Talking to herself, she goes;
and outdoors a cold wind blows,

cold against her face, and wild—
"God, protect my only child!"

Strange house, full of folk. The boy's
motionless; he makes no noise,
asks for nothing, never speaks,
no one's heard him laugh in weeks.
Not of day or night he takes
notice; neither sleeps nor wakes.
Vassilka—a strange new name—
strikes his little heart with pain.

Mother roams about; she's grown,
like her son, as still as stone.
No one knows, and no one cares.
Waits and waits—too well compares
with Jochebed, Moses' mother!
For, abandoned as that other
to the mercy of the Nile,
she has left her only child.

Isaac Katzenelson
(1886–1944)

*Born in 1886 in Karelitz, Byelorussia, Isaac Katzenelson moved to War-
saw as a boy. He worked for the Hebrew newspaper* Hazefirah, *and
was first published at sixteen. Later he wrote several well-received plays,
including* The Prophet *and* The White Life. *For some years he directed
a Hebrew-Polish high school in Lodz. He was a Hebrew writer, but when
Hitler seized Poland, driving the Jews into ghettos and death camps, he
turned to Yiddish. With a false passport he was admitted to France in
1943, but he was interned in the Vittel concentration camp and ulti-
mately deported to Auschwitz, where he perished. After the war, the
manuscript of his "Song of the Slaughtered Jewish People," along with
other of his Yiddish poems in manuscript, was discovered in three hermeti-
cally sealed bottles in the hollow of an old tree in the Vittel camp. It
aroused wide attention and was published in several languages, includ-
ing German.*

The Song of the Slaughtered Jewish People
(excerpt)

I looked out of the window and beheld the hands that struck;
observed who did the beating up, and who were beaten up;
and wrung my hands for very shame . . . oh mockery and shame:
It was by Jews, alas, by Jews my Jewish folk was slain!

Apostates, half-apostates, with a shiny-booted tread,
with hats whose Star of David looked like swastikas instead;
a language strange and awkward in their mouths, and mean and
    fierce,
they dragged us from our dwelling places, pitched us down the stairs.

They tore the doors down, tore inside with curses and commands;
invaded Jewish homes with clubs held ready in their hands;
found us and beat us, bullied us to where the wagons stood—
both young and old! And soiled the light of day, and spat at God.

They dragged us from beneath our beds, from closets, with a curse:
"The wagon's waiting! Go to hell! or death! whichever's worse!"
They dragged us out into the street and then went back to forage:
one final dress, one final slice of bread, one sip of porridge.

And on the street—a spectacle to drive you mad: the street
has perished, and with one tremendous clamor, one great shriek,
the street—way up and way, way down—is empty and—is teeming
with wagons full of Jews! just look—with wagons full of
    screaming . . .

Wagons of Jews! Some of them wring their hands, some tear their
    hair,
and some are silent—ah! That silence is too loud to bear!
They look about . . . Is it an evil dream? Or is it true?
And round the wagons—booted, hatted—Herr Policeman Jew!

The German stands apart, as if he's laughing at the scene—
the German keeps his distance—has no need to come between;
ah, woe is me! he's managed it! by Jews my Jews are slain!
Behold the wagons! Ah, behold the agony, the shame!

Chaieh Ledik

A Bit of Bread

Yellow patch across my back;
on my shoulder an empty pack.
When at last the coast is clear,
we girls are ready to take wing:
deserted cellars, full of things,
wait for us to appear.

Eyes of fear
inspect each nook.
Searching here, searching there,
we dash from cellar to cellar, look
for something, something—till we're led
through the gloom to a bit of bread.

(sung in a camp near Bremen)

Lerke Rosenblum

The poet, a young girl, escaped from a German concentration camp.

I Yearn

I yearn for the laugh, free and open,
that long ago rang through the air;
an uproar of children, unbroken
by motherless sobs of despair.

I yearn for a step to be taken
with pride and a sense of self-worth.
I yearn for the day when I'll waken
to find myself free on the earth.

(Kovno Ghetto)

S. Shenker

The Grief-Stricken Heart

Why is my heart so wrenched with grief
yet not one tear can flow?
And life is always dark for me
no matter where I go?

Why is the sun not here today
to warm me with its glare?
I have no garment, after all,
nor any shoes to wear.

And am I fatherless as well?
without a mother too?
Where are you, brothers, sisters all—
are any left of you?

O why, despite my grief, have I
not one more tear to shed?
Perhaps because the time has come
for Kaddish to be said.

(Kovno Ghetto)

Moishe Shimmel

(1903–   )

Moishe Shimmel, born in Lemberg in 1903, moved to Warsaw in 1930. Immersing himself in Polish literature, he produced three volumes of verse in Polish between 1931 and 1935. But in 1930 he began writing Yiddish poems as well, and was included in the 1940 Kiev anthology Soviet Literature. *His only Yiddish collection,* I'm Lonely, *was issued in 1937. Trapped in the Lemberg ghetto and perhaps later in the Warsaw ghetto, he is believed to have escaped to Byelorussia in 1941. The circumstances of his death are unknown.*

To a Little Boy

Don't cry, little boy, wipe your tears, things will yet be good.
We shall yet heal the wounds that are dripping blood.

We stand alone in the world against the sun's vanishing glow;
alone, alone with our poverty and with our woe.

We've got to find some consolation, we ourselves:
repair the doors, just you and I, put up the walls, the shelves.

Let them come to thrash us, rob us of the little that remains,
we'll patch our cushions again, install new windowpanes.

Once, and a second, a third time, until the yearned-for last;
we're patient, we can wait, until their time is passed.

Be quiet, little boy, dry your tears and weep no more;
we'll repair the chairs and table; we'll redo the floor.

We'll reconstruct the house that they set fire to;
the ruined walls will glitter in the sun anew.

Don't cry, little boy, don't spoil your eyes, bright days are at hand.
Spring will find its way back to us in the end.

Because the hand will be hacked down, like an old rotten stem,
the hand that seized your father and mother and slaughtered them.

Eternity

I need help like a person dangerously ailing.
I want to flee the dusk, the sunlight failing.
I seek a kinship with the grasses and the snow.
Do I dare hope that out of them I'll grow?
But screaming does not help, and hurts me so . . .

I fall to Earth with yearning and with glee;
I look for a resemblance between her and me;
but she's enormous, and exudes eternity.
I tap the table, tap the wall, the sill—
but it's no good: I'm dangerously ill;
night after night the sunset haunts my bed.
Just to admit it, makes my face burn red:
—because I'm scared of being dead.

Joshua Zendorf
(1902–)

Born in Lodz on May 19, 1902, Zendorf attended yeshiva and then became a printer. He devoted himself to revolutionary activities and was forced to flee Poland. Settling in Danzig, he produced a volume of poems, Red Commands, *in 1937. On May 14, 1941, he was deported from Paris to the concentration camp of Petivia and, some time later, was shipped to Auschwitz. The following verses, written and sung in Petivia, were afterward transmitted by the poet's widow, Stella, to her brother-in-law in Lodz.*

Our Spirit Is Not Broken

No, our spirit is not broken,
and the earth's a lovely place.
Victory has been bespoken
over everything that's base.

    See the world—once more it's blooming,
    as it's done each year, each May.
    Jew and non-Jew, fellow human,
    once our chains are torn away.

Each once more will be united
with his children, with his wife.
Spirits high and hearts ignited,
we'll restore the golden life.

It's too old a story, drumming
hatred between Christian, Jew.
Times of wickedness are coming,
yet for all the grass is new.

Higher than the barracks, loud
and clear be lifted our refrain.

For us all, the field is ploughed;
and for us all grows ripe the grain!

> See the world—once more it's blooming,
> as it's done each year, each May.
> Jew and non-Jew, fellow human,
> once our chains are torn away!

Partisan Poets

In *The Penguin Book of Modern Yiddish Verse,* Irving Howe calls Vilna "one of the most vital Jewish communities of eastern Europe." A third of its inhabitants were Jews when Hitler struck. Inspired by the brilliant poet Moishe Kulbak, a cluster of gifted and politically advanced young writers formed Young Vilna in the early 1930s, published their own vibrant books and journals, and established worldwide literary contacts. Two of their most promising members fled east ahead of the Nazi onslaught. Leizer Wolf, most of whose poems have not survived, starved to death near Samarkand. Chaim Grade lived through the war in Soviet refuge, but his family stayed behind and were slaughtered.

It is not surprising that a particularly vigorous partisan movement developed in the forests outside Vilna, and that among its members were the Young Vilna poets whose work follows, along with Leah Rudnitsky, author of the dearly loved, untranslatably harrowing lullaby, "Birds Are Drowsing in the Branches." What contributions might have been made by Vilna's Leib Apeskin, Leah Rudnitsky, and Hirsh Glik—murdered at twenty-two—along with Bialystok's splendid young Jack Gordon, only a handful of whose poems were recovered, can be imagined when one considers the achievements of those partisan-poets who survived: the great anthologist-historian Shmerke Katcherginsky, and Avrom Sutzkever, who ripened spectacularly into a giant of the century.

Leib Apeskin
(1908–1944)

Leib Apeskin was born in Vilna in 1908 and was trained there as a teacher of Yiddish. He was imprisoned by the Polish authorities for revolutionary activities. In the Vilna ghetto he lectured, involved himself in the school movement, and translated songs for choral use. Among his own songs were "Dawn," "Tramp, Tramp, Tramp," and "On the Death of the Teacher Gerstein." In 1939, he was published in Soviet-Yiddish journals and was afterward among the founders of the partisan organization. He is said to have assembled a collection of his songs; when Vilna was liberated, partisans found a bloody bundle of his songs beside his body. He was killed on July 11, 1944.

Why Was It So Bright?

Why, yesterday, was it so bright overhead?
and why did each street look so gay?
and why should the sun that was radiant, red,
be clouded and angry today?

The heavens, the house, and the street are now crying;
the heart, in its silence, grieves on.
Can someone forget, if he tries and keeps trying,
the hours of joy that are gone?

Away with your teardrops, away with your sorrow!
To grieve cannot do any good.
Perhaps by tomorrow—yes, surely tomorrow—
the sun will burst forth as it should!

Shmerke Katcherginsky

(1908–1955)

Born in Vilna in 1908, Shmerke Katcherginsky was orphaned early and brought up by his grandfather. He became a lithographer. Active in the Communist underground, he was arrested several times. Under the pseudonym of Ch. Shmerke he contributed to Young Vilna *from 1934 to 1936. When the Soviet Union gave Vilna to Lithuania, he left with the Red Army and taught in the Bialystok area, returning when the Soviets took all of Lithuania in 1940. After the Nazi invasion, he wandered about his homeland disguised as a deaf-mute, but entered the Vilna ghetto in 1942 as a cultural activist and partisan. Along with Sutzkever, he rescued many priceless Jewish treasures from the Nazis, hiding them in a bunker. A year later, he fled to the forests and fought as a partisan, returning to his city when the Red Army liberated it in July 1944. Disappointed in the Soviet attitude toward the revival of Jewish culture, he left for Lodz in 1946; there he served on the Central Jewish Historical Commission and completed his first anthology,* Our Songs. *After the pogroms at Kielce, he moved to Paris, where in 1947 his* Songs of the Vilna Ghetto, The Destruction of Vilna, *and* Partisans on the Move *were published. These were followed by the massive anthology* Songs of the Ghettos, *with a foreword by H. Leivick, and* Between the Hammer and Sickle, *a study of the Soviet attack on Jewish culture. He settled in Buenos Aires in 1950, and his autobiography,* I Was a Partisan, *appeared there two years later. He died in an air crash in 1955 while on a fund-raising tour for the Jewish National Fund. The same year, a Shmerke Katcherginsky Memorial Volume was issued. "Spring," his most touching song, with music by A. Brudno, was written after the death in April 1943 of his wife, Barbara (born in Cracow). It was sung first as part of a Little Art Stage production by Rochel, sister of the young partisan-poet Leah Rudnitsky, and later in other ghettos, death camps, and partisan encampments. Here is the opening stanza:*

> I'm led by my feet
> from street unto street
> and can't find a place for my grief;
> my darling is gone,
> how does one go on?—

good friends, grant one word of relief.
The home that I live in
is lit up by heaven—
what comfort is that for me? None.
A beggar, I wait
before every gate
and beg—for a droplet of sun.

Warsaw
(written in the woods of Narotch, January 18, 1944,
to commemorate the anniversary of the first Warsaw uprising)

The night does not pass and the day does not dawn.
The earth is a planet gone bloody.
A Jew flutters up like a flag in the storm,
a flag in the valley of bodies.

In ruins the ghetto; its Jews—in a fight.
Through fire he strides past his brothers.
"Take vengeance! Take vengeance!" he storms at the night—
"for children, for fathers, for mothers!"

The earth does not whiten, though snow falls and falls:
the blood goes on crimsonly writing—
it covers the whiteness—for vengeance it calls—
the blood of the Jews who died fighting.

"There won't come a day," cries the Jew, "nor a night!
The nations will not be forgiven!
Whoever among us went down in the fight,
in us will forever be living!

"Inspired, we'll think of the dangers they braved;
we'll reckon the sorrows that wrenched them.
Let three cries of blood in your heart be engraved:
Avenge them! Avenge them! Avenge them!"

Ballad of Itzik Wittenberg

The enemy hearkens: a beast in the darkness;
the Mauser—it wakes in my hand—
but wait! my heart's drumming: two sentries are coming,
and with them our first-in-command.

The ghetto is sundered by lightning and thunder;
"Beware!" shrieks a tower in fright.
Brave fighters have freed our commander and leader
and fled with him into the night.

But night soon is over—and death lies uncovered;
the flames of the city leap high.
Aroused is the ghetto—the storm troopers threaten:
"Give up your leader, or die!"

The battleground quivers as Itzik delivers
the answer—while guns hold their breath:
"Shall others be given, to pay for my living?"
And proudly he goes to his death.

Once more in the darkness the enemy hearkens;
the Mauser—it wakes in my hand.
You are now dearer—now you be my hero!
Now you be my first-in-command!

Avrom Sutzkever

(1913–   )

Born in Smorgon, near Vilna, on June 15, 1913, Avrom Sutzkever and his family escaped the pogroms of World War I by moving to Omsk, Siberia. At seven he witnessed his father's fatal heart attack. Two years later his mother brought her family back, first to their ruined town, then to Vilna, where her gifted five-year-old daughter died. In his early teens Sutzkever became a serious poet, especially influenced by Moishe Leib Halpern, and he joined Young Vilna. Siberia *(1937) was his first major work. During World War II, his mother and his newborn baby were among the slaughtered, but he survived—first by hiding in the Vilna sewers, later as a partisan in the forests. Along with his comrade S. Katcherginsky, he succeeded in gradually rescuing, at extreme personal risk, a large part of Vilna's centuries-old YIVO treasury. Amazingly, night after night, the young poet turned his anguish, his despair, and gradually his sense of indestructibility, into stanzas of the most excruciatingly shimmering loveliness. As if single-handedly piecing together the shattered alphabet of his people, he expanded the possibilities of Yiddish prosody beyond what were thought to be their limits.*

At one and the same time he had transformed himself into an incomparable virtuoso and a pure folk-balladeer, whose singing kept himself and Vilna's spirit alive, and who avenged the horrors of each day with pen and rifle. The poems he created during those years, including the epic Secret Town, *"succeeded," according to Jacob Glatstein, "in presenting in the purest form the greatest horror of all time." He later testified at the Nuremberg war crimes trials. Since the late 1940s he has lived in Israel, editing the distinguished quarterly* Golden Chain *and producing extraordinary volumes of both poetry and prose, including* In the Fire Chariot, Ode to the Dove, *and* Songs from the Sea of Death, *a 480-page compilation of all his Holocaust poetry.* The First Night in the Ghetto, Poems 1941–1944, *though written at the time, did not appear in print until 1979. Sutzkever, ever-ripening, looms among the century's outstanding literary figures, a worthy Nobel candidate if ever there was one. But neither that as yet unawarded prize, nor any he has received, could compare with the response those in the Vilna Ghetto must have given when they first heard his ballad of their beloved teacher, Mira, on the night of May 10, 1943. That poem is here included.*

In the Dungeon

As always: the gloom wants to smother me quite.
The lead-colored rodents all gnaw at my sight.
I enter the dungeon and sink underground—
if one thing that's human, one shred, could be found!

I come on a fragment of glass, in whose clutches
a moonbeam in glazen captivity twitches.
My sinking's forgot in a flame of elation:
This thing, after all, was a human creation!

Along its glass sharpness I fondle the moon:
"You want it? I'll give you my life as a boon!"
But life's very warm, and the glass very cold
to thrust at a throat less than thirty years old.

(Vilna, end of June 1941)

My Mother
(concluding sections)

I look for the precious four walls
where you drew breath;

behind me the stairs disappear
like a water hole steaming.

I reach for the knob, and tear
the door to your life—

it's as if a little bird weeps
in the cage of my fingers.

I enter the room in which
your dream's growing dark—

scarcely flickers the lamp
you lately lighted.

On the table a glass of tea
you did not quite sip;

fingers still quiver about
on the rims of silver . . .

"Have mercy!" begs the tongue
of flame in the lamp—

I feed the lamp with my blood
to keep it from dying.

.   .   .

Not you do I find, but your smock—ripped apart.
I hold it ashamedly pressed to my heart.
The holes in your smock are the days of my life
and the seam of it runs through my heart like a knife.

I tear off my clothing and creep in your bare,
thin garment as if in myself. What I wear
no more is a smock; it's your radiant skin,
your death, left behind, I am shuddering in.

.   .   .

You speak to me,
and your voice rings true:
"Don't do it, my child;
it's sinful, it's wild;
accept as rightful
my parting from you.

"While you have breath
I too exist—
as the pit in the plum
contains what will come:
tree, nest, robin,
and all the rest."

(Vilna Ghetto, October 1942)

The Lost Roses
(from "The Three Roses")

I'll go off to seek you; a shovel I'll bring
to tunnel through graves, plough up meadow and farm;
I'll question the grasses and let the thorn sting;
and always your shadow will lean on my arm.

And if, after all, you are not to be found,
I'll dig into words and I'll plough every sound,
until the lost roses are freed from the ground,
that kingdom of night in whose deeps they were drowned.

(Vilna Ghetto, October 1942)

Before Night

In rows, in battalions, they shuffle, they crowd;
I see them no longer, but feel every tread.
Like birds when their flutter is screened by a cloud,
each shape, with a sound of its own, moves ahead.

The line stretches on through my vision, through me,
and each finds his dream there—the self he'd not known.
At last in the light of my blindness I see
how many the souls that have merged in my own.

(Vilna Ghetto, January 10, 1943)

The Teacher Mira

With patches of yellow to cover our bones,
past all our old streets, to the ghetto we're driven.
Each house says goodbye to its daughters, its sons,
and stone-faced we greet each command that is given.

Phylacteries crown every grandfather's head;
a calf and a cottager, paired from the start;
one drags by her nails a beloved, half-dead,
another—a bundle of wood on a cart.

And right in the midst of them, Mira the teacher—
a child on one arm, like a bright golden zither;
and safe in her handclasp a second bright creature;
and pupils, battalions of them, always with her.

A gate's at the old Jewish quarter, its wood
as warm as a corpse that seems merely asleep;
and just like a sluice for some swift-driven flood
it opens, and swallows them into the deep.

They're chased without light, without bread, through the rubble;
a pencil's their light and a book is their bread.
She finds them a ruined apartment; with double
devotion to Mira their work moves ahead.

The children both sparkle and laugh as she reads them
a story by Sholom Aleichem; their hair
she tenderly combs, with blue ribbons she braids them,
and counts: a full hundred and thirty are there.

The teacher awakes with the sun; as it mounts,
she waits for the children, the life of her life.
They come. And she counts them. O, best not to count!
A score, overnight, were cut down by the knife.

Her face is a pane that the dusk madly streaks;
but never like this must the children behold her!
So, biting her lip with new courage, she speaks
of Leckert;* the boldness of him makes them bolder.

At midnight a grayness has quilted each yard,
and with it the hair of the teacher turns gray:
the cellar! She looks for her mother, looks hard—
with seventeen children she's vanished away.

When sun dried the blood, Mira silently hung
her orphaned apartment with green bits of spirit;
—came Gerstein the teacher: "Our song must be sung
so loudly that over the gates they can hear it!"

It rings forth: "The spring is not far." Under ax
and sword thrust, the groundworks of tenements quiver.
They're dragged by the hair from the cellars and cracks.
"The spring is not far!" rings out louder than ever.

Now—sisterless, motherless—sixty are left.
She's mother, she's sister: My darlings, my doves—
a holiday's coming; we've got to be swift—
let's put on a program that everyone loves!

At show-time just forty remain. But each one—
with little white shirt, and with such a bright look.
The stage is transformed: there's a garden, a sun . . .
You almost can go for a dip in the brook.

*Hirsh Leckert, a martyred young labor leader.

But just as the Third Gift of Peretz * was rendered,
catastrophe tore like a saw through their haven.
The enemy pounced! and by dawn, of a hundred
and thirty, there lived only Mira and seven.

And so, till her senses were split by the blade,
the children were—bees, and their teacher—a flower.
The flower's gone gray and her limbs have decayed,
but tall in the dew of the dawn she will tower!

(Vilna Ghetto, May 10, 1943)

A Sword with Wings

In dream and in reality you sent the Lord of Woe
unto me, and declared: Pay what you owe!
But I cried out in welcome, as is best:
O blessed guest!

And I stripped bare my flesh and my fleshed word for him to see:
Subdue thy passion; I am pledged to thee!
In through my limbs' coat, open to the sight,
sow thy great light!

And if I'm filled, how slight my pain beside the flood of pains!
Instead of lamentation—godly aims.
They burn away my weakness, turn me, Lord,
into a sword.

And now, when raging at the world, I am a sword with wings.
Your face, reflected in its metal, streams.
It was the Lord of Woe who made my dower
this awesome power.

(Vilna Ghetto, May 20, 1943)

---

*Peretz's great short story, "Three Gifts."

Song of a Jewish Poet in 1943

Am I, then, of all Europe's poets, the last?
With no one but corpses and vultures to listen?
In fire, in swamp, I am drowning—held fast
by yellow, patched hours as if in a prison.

I bite at my hours with the teeth of a beast
made strong by a tear of my mother's. I see
the million-pulsed heart of my brothers deceased
who rise from the ground and are rushing at me.

The million-pulsed heart—that am I! I'm assigned
to shelter the songs left behind when they fell.
And God, since His temples were razed by mankind,
I hide in myself, like the sun in a well.

Be open, my heart! See them burst into bloom,
those heavenly hours the future holds dear!
O strengthen their purpose, and make them come soon,
and be, in your sorrow, their trumpet, their seer!

And sing of the swamps, till a tear of your mother's
has welled once again! Give your voice to the breeze,
and let it be heard by the bones of your brothers,
the ghetto ablaze, and your kin overseas!

(Vilna Ghetto, June 22, 1943)

If No Trace of My People Shall Be Found

If no trace of my people shall be found,
I pray it: From my memory disappear!
And let all graves sink deeper underground.
And let no dust remain of month or year.

And to my rifle this is what I say:
Within my hand may you become a snake,

if those unborn, those of a brighter day,
don't hear the shot I am about to take.

(the woods of Narotch, January 30, 1944)

Let Each Be a Fortress!

Rage in the bells of the conscience that's deaf,
you right-loving knight of the tower!
Let each be a fortress, opposing himself
to the iron storm of this hour.

Like coals let the long-smothered spirit be fanned,
though hope refuses to beckon.
Without ever quaking must wake in the hand
our holy Jewish weapon!

(Vilna Ghetto, July 14, 1943)

Don't Sing the Sorrowful

Don't sing the sorrowful;
don't bring disgrace
upon sorrow.
Words are treacherous;
they'll about-face
tomorrow.

Look at the snow;
in its calm let your memory be
illuminated:
light is your heart's language. And you—
are re-
created.

Toward the snow, the icy fleece,
your fingers are bidden
to reach.

One touch—you release
the life that is hidden
in each.

(the woods of Narotch, February 5, 1944)

The Third Hand

The chopped-off hand that I discovered once upon a time
by the tomatoes in the garden rightfully is mine.
And since it is a man's hand with no owner of its own,
it's mine. A third hand, without which I set not one word down.

To curious readers—ten or so—I candidly admit:
it isn't I who feed them words of witchery and wit.
Into the paper's ear a stranger's recollection came:
my third hand, found by the tomatoes, is to blame.

To read that script it's not enough to know the Yiddish tongue.
I teach myself its language. Wander all alone among
its winding trailways late at night and fall on stones and thorns,
and see it in the seeds by the tomatoes when it dawns.

The hand that may have fondled a young woman at the time
they hacked its owner into bits—the chopped-off hand is mine.
I found it when he lost it, when it lay there claimed by none
by the tomatoes in September Nineteen Forty-One.

Jacob (Jack) Gordon
(1916–1943)

Jacob (Jack) Gordon was born in Bialystok, around 1916. His first verses appeared in Awakener of Youth *(1936, Warsaw). Later poems were included in Nachman Maisel's Warsaw journal* Literary Leaves. *He died (c. 1943) as a partisan in the forests around Bialystok; after the war several of his poems were unearthed in the Bialystok ghetto. His talent is clearly of a high order, and his early death is an incalculable loss to Yiddish poetry.*

The Bridge Reverberates Each Step We Take

The bridge reverberates each step we take.
We stop a while and look below:
a train flies through, and here comes one in its wake,
and people nod at them hurtling through.
Just as they're standing now, I once stood there
spruced-up in bright new sailor-shirt and shorts.
My father with his fingers combed my hair
and promised to send chocolates and tortes.
The train's hoot mocked his hopes and plans.
You stand near me and fix your eyes
on me, and mine fix inward. I can feel your hands—
my throat senses your palm, my heart can recognize
your fingers. You're playing with me—and I'm
your child. Who told us love would be waving
more fiercely here on this bridge at this time
than the wind in the field—when the hoot of the train,
so fatefully harsh, wakes a tenfold craving
for joy? But here, where your hand slides over my skin,
tomorrow a bayonet will kiss me.
The hoot of the train, the roar of my fate,
caress, oh caress me . . .
It's dark, it's late.

While Carrying Loads of Timber

While carrying loads of timber
we laughed at a certain grotesque;
whenever the log on his shoulders rocked
he kept his eyelids pressed;
lids pressed tight and pale lips locked,
he quietly came along
not seeing the steps he was taking.
He tripped in the grass more often than not,
log rocking and twisting, while we—
we laughed—and for what?
Now, when the darkness runs out of me
and my memories waken,
I finally see:
it was at our own selves we were making
mock, to smother
the sob within the heart,
because like that log-bent brother
our spirit had become:
ashamed, inert,
in a filthy shirt,
with burdens that spurt from clumsy hands,
with footstep weary, numb.

And Have There Been Many More Days Allotted?

And have there been many more days allotted?
A certain foreboding works in my blood—
the way I exist is not good, is not good.
I raise my hand: it is heavy, clayey;
I trudge as if out of a swamp somewhere,
and the distance is clouded, forbidden, and bare,
and leaving is not in my power.
Then is this hour
the last? Is this the way it closes,
as at the threshold of our burned-out houses:
—broken, forlorn,
with a heart so empty, so sick, so worn
that vengeance no longer burns as its goal?

In the final hour—
        make strong my soul!

Hirsh Glik
(1922–1944)

Hirsh Glik was born in Vilna in 1922. His father dealt in scrap iron, rags, and used bottles. From early youth the poet belonged to Hashomer Hatzair (The Young Guard). He began writing Hebrew verses in 1935 but turned to Yiddish under the influence of the Young Vilna group. He formed a writers' group of his own among the neighborhood children. The poet Leizer Wolf (whose powerful lullaby is in this volume) became their mentor. Glik had left school at sixteen to work in a book bindery and a paper factory, but a year later, under Leizer Wolf's guidance, he and his young circle managed to produce a journal of their own, Young Forest. *When the Nazis took Vilna, he and his father were among those sent to do forced labor in the peat bogs fifteen miles from the city. He became sick there but continued inspiring the hundreds around him with his new songs, which reached Vilna and won great popularity. Among these songs were "The Ballad of the Brown Theater" and "Typhus Ballad." Because the peat-bog workers were in contact with the partisans, the camp was liquidated in May 1943; Glik was sent back to the ghetto, where he continued writing songs. In October, the ghetto itself was liquidated; he tried to join the partisans in the forests, but the Gestapo caught him and shipped him to the concentration camp at Goldfield. He perished in 1944. The first song that follows, loved as much for its haunting melody as for the words, was written after the initial diversionary action of the partisans near Vilna, where Itzik Matzkevich and Vitke Kempner blew up a German echelon. The second song became at once, and has remained, the anthem of the Resistance.*

Not a Sound; the Night Is Starry

Not a sound; the night is starry,
and the frost—a burning brand.
Remember: I taught you how to carry
a gun, how to grip it in your hand!

A girl, beret and fur piece matching,
crouches with pistol in her clasp.

A girl with a face of velvet, watching
the enemy's caravan go past.

Her little gun takes aim at their position
and fires once, and finds its mark.
A car full of arms and ammunition
she stops with a bullet in the dark!

Creep forth from the woods at day's beginning,
a snow-crown garlanding our hair;
one little triumph now, but sure of winning
the liberty for which we die and dare!

Partisan Song

Never say that there is only death for you,
though leaden skies may be concealing days of blue,
because the hour that we have hungered for is near;
beneath our tread the earth shall tremble: "We are here!"

From land of palm tree to the far-off land of snow
we shall be coming with our torment, with our woe;
and everywhere our blood has sunk into the earth
shall our bravery, our vigor, blossom forth . . .

We'll have the morning sun to set our day aglow,
and all our yesterdays shall vanish with the foe.
And if the time is long before the sun appears,
then let this song go like a signal through the years.

This song was written with our blood, and not with lead;
it's not a song that summer birds sing overhead;
it was a people, among toppling barricades,
that sang this song of ours with pistols and grenades.

So never say that there is only death for you.
Leaden skies may be concealing days of blue;
yet the hour that we have hungered for is near;
beneath our tread the earth shall tremble: "We are here!"

Soviet Yiddish Poets

"Babi-Yar" and "Cradlesong," the harrowing Shike Driz lullabies included in this volume, are a sufficient reminder of Hitler's colossal extermination campaign against Soviet Jews. Driz (1908–71), a Red Army volunteer, served in Galician border towns from 1939 to 1941, aiding many refugees from the Nazis as well as local Jewish villagers.

Moishe Broderson's "A New Lullaby" introduces a Red Army soldier such as Shike Driz, away at war, whose wife has been killed and whose little daughter sits alone rocking her doll. Broderson (1890–1956), though born in Moscow and brought up in a Byelorussian town, lived in Lodz for twenty years. In 1939, he fled east before the Nazi invaders. Imprisoned along with most of his fellow poets in 1948, he survived the executions of 1952 and was banished instead to a Siberian slave-labor camp, from which he was freed in 1955. A year later he died in Warsaw.

These three lullabies, and the handful of poems that follow, are but a glimpse of the response by Soviet Yiddish poets to the decimation of their people.

David Hofshtein
(1889–1952)

Born in Karostichev, near Kiev, in 1889, the son of a farmer, David Hofshtein wrote his first poem in Hebrew at nine. Later he wrote in Russian and Ukrainian as well. At seventeen he taught in a nearby village. After army service, he attended Kiev's Commercial Institute and studied philology at the University of Kiev. It was not until 1917 that he wrote and published in Yiddish. Two years later, his first collection, Along the Roads, *was issued. Under attack for signing a protest against the suppression of Hebrew, he went to Berlin in 1923, leaving behind his motherless sons. His collection* Wall Panels *appeared there. Two years later, he moved to Palestine, but returned home in 1926 and was "rehabilitated." Many books followed, including* Selected Poems *(1931),* Orchestra *(1933), and* In Our Days *(1939). The same year, with Itzik Feffer, he edited* Nations Sing, *and in 1940 he coedited Mayakovsky's* Poems. *In the decades from 1919 to 1939 he also translated major works by Andreyev, Upton Sinclair, Henri Barbusse, Pushkin, Schiller, and Shevchenko. In honor of his fiftieth birthday, his poems were issued in Russian translation. A war volume,* I Believe, *appeared in 1944. The poems that follow are from that collection. Two years later, the government gave him a medal for heroism during the war. His* Selected Works *were published in 1948. The same year he was arrested, but— according to Moishe Broderson's widow—went insane and could therefore not be shot with his brother-poets. He died later in the prison's mental ward. A volume of his poems in Russian translation was issued in 1958.*

No Weeping!

And I passed and beheld you wallowing in your blood,
and I said: In your blood, live! And I said:
In your blood, live! —Ezekiel

I see—
you are wholly in blood.
I see
that your forehead is plastered with dirt.

146

I tell you:
No weeping! remember—
your mind is alive, is unhurt!
and through anguish, through woe
comes, as ever, creation, the glow.
I know—
there are bruises enough on your body,
and your heart carries wounds without number—
you are battered and bloody . . .
I tell you:
No weeping! remember—
your strength is alive, is entire!
Your heart, beating still, still afire,
drives your will, your desire,
and is lifted by fortitude still!
And your hand, your trained hand with its manifold skill
(which Rembrandt portrayed),
has mastered the deadliest blade,
the most delicate tool.
I know that your burden is heavy, so heavy and cruel!
But your mission is grand—
no matter how hard are these years,
endure your distress without tears!
Step outside
and shout:
World in, world out!
Uncowed by the ways
of the world, to plant your feet wide
and stand
and survive—
pays!

Spring

Far too wild is this day's wonder,
and for once I can't surrender;
it should make me brave and cheerful,
but instead I'm glum and fearful.

Very different is the way
I respond to spring today:
I approach this morning's splendor
as if to some evil wonder.

Though the day displays its power,
yet the sun that hour by hour
climbs the sky has seen those homes,
seen those holes like gaping groans;

yet the sun, on its bright path,
has lit up Destruction, Death,
shown them every house and barn
marked for horror, marked for harm;

yet the sun's impartial beam
did not hesitate to gleam
upon faces turning yellow,
upon eyes burnt out and hollow!

on all people, no exception;
lavishing its benediction
on the young and old who died,
and the jaws of genocide.

"People"—at the word I freeze;
people—I'm not one of these!
for I live, I still draw breath,
and I do not deal in death.

I'm no corpse, nor have I killed;
my commission is to shield;
but my weapons—only words—
and I'm so dismayed, it hurts—

and my hand's a frail defender,
and the sun's an evil wonder.

Leib Kvitko

(1890–1952)

Leib Kvitko was born in Oleskovo, the Ukraine, in 1890, the son of a teacher. Orphaned when very young, he was brought up by his grandfather and had to earn his living at the age of ten. Two years later he began writing verse, but it was not until 1918 that his work was printed. In 1919, his first book, Step, *was published. From 1922 to 1925, he worked at his government's Hamburg mission. He lived in Kharkov from 1926 to 1936, active in the revival of Yiddish theater and on the staff of the journal* Red World. *In 1929, after the publication of* Struggles, 1917– 1929, *he came under attack by the Proletarian Writers Group, Russia's equivalent of the Proletpen. Stripped of his editorial post, he became a tractor worker. In 1936 he moved to Moscow, and three years later was awarded the Red Worker's Banner. The same year his book* New Poems *was issued. His works achieved immense popularity and were published in huge editions in many Soviet languages. Prior to his arrest in 1948, he produced two more volumes:* Songs That Suit My Mood *(1947) and* Selected Works *(1948). He was among those murdered in prison in August 1952. One of Kvitko's collections,* Early Years, *holds a special place as a direct victim of the Holocaust. About to be issued in 1941, its printing was destroyed by Nazi bombs. It was finally published in Moscow in 1984. The first poem that follows was written in 1942, a year of extraordinary devastation and even more extraordinary resistance in the poet's homeland.*

Strength

The rock is strong—
but steel will crack it.
The steel is strong—
but flame will wreck it.
The flame is strong—
but the stream buries it.
The stream is strong—
but the cloud carries it.
The cloud is strong—

but the wind drives it.
The wind is strong—
but man survives it.
The man is strong—
but death fells him.
Death is strong—
but glory quells him:
Who offers our need
his blood, his breath,
his glorious deed—
is stronger than death.

Before

We hove up walls for work and home,
and planted roses, watched them grow.
Alive as dancers, to and fro,
with mattocks bitingly aglow
we lifted rock, we lifted loam.

We learned to lessen mankind's pain,
explored the galaxies, and gave
our children pleasure, made them brave,
woke lust for learning in their brain.

And yet that grim affliction found us
just as our sun was at its height.
And children wept and wailed in fright;
southland and north in flight, in flight!
Death followed, flung his arms around us.

The Word about Ethel

I swear to keep it in my memory for all time,
till judgment is at last pronounced on the last crime;
I swear my testimony then will be presented
for this same little child, the mocked one, the tormented.

For her, the cobbler's Ethel of the radiant brow,
harnessed at eight years old to history's harsh plough;
torn from her dolls, her merry voice stopped up by cares,
and on her back the burden of six thousand years.

No longer is she Ethel, Ethel of the dark bright eyes,
but "Yude"; "Yude dog!" her persecutor cries.
For centuries she's baked her matzoh with Christ's blood
and been a part of the world bankers' brotherhood.

That's why she hides in wildernesses now, in ditches,
to keep from being snared and slain by heartless wretches.
At night, in fever-dread, she creeps with other children
toward Russia, but the German guards would catch and kill them.

Her head, her throat, whose beauty Solomon once knew,
are brutalized by scabies now; only her dreams
search in the downpour, as the dove of Noah flew
seeking a dry place; in her eyes are Abel's screams.

No, no, I can't, I'm not allowed to let it fade.
Neither with tears nor outcries can such woe be weighed.
Crawl to me, let me clasp you close as one should do;
Ethel, dear child, what has the monster made of you?

He's turned the world you loved into an ugly place;
he's wracked its face with ulcers, like your mother's face.
I want to see: How are you looking at it, Girl?
Dear Ethel, let me help you not to hate the world . . .

Peretz Markish
(1895–1952)

Born in 1895 in Polnoe, Volhynia, Peretz Markish began writing Russian poetry at fifteen. He joined the army in 1916, fought on the German front, and was wounded. A year later, his first Yiddish poems were published. Kvitko, Hofshtein, and Bergelson joined him in founding the Kiev School of writers in 1918; with the publication of their anthology Eigens (Our Own), *Soviet Yiddish literature was born. From that time until his sojourn in Poland three years later, he produced five volumes of poetry, beginning with* Thresholds. *In Warsaw, with Uri-Zvi Greenberg, Ravitch, and Zeitlin, he moved Yiddish poetry into exuberant and shocking new paths; they defiantly accepted the contemptuous epithet of "Khaliastre" (The Gang) as their name. In Paris, he coedited the anthology* Khaliastre. *In 1926, he returned to his homeland;* The Brothers *appeared three years later, and* Selected Poems *in 1933. The Spanish civil war inspired* Poems for Spain *(1938), but it was the anti-Hitler struggle that called forth his greatest responses, culminating in the epic* War, *published in 1948, and a huge novel,* March of Generations. *Along with many other Yiddish writers he was imprisoned in 1948, and was murdered on August 12, 1952. His* Works *were issued in a two-volume Russian edition in 1960.*

To a Jewish Dancer
(excerpt)

Will you, my homeless one, try once again your wings?
Is there some road that does not know your sufferings?
Brisk* has unlocked herself like an old book of prayer,
and multitudes come thronging in with their despair.

On foot, backs bent, they bring their children from afar.
Their beards—upturned. Their wander-guide—the stars.
Their exile—knotted by their prayer-belts round the loins,
parchmented foreheads straining to translate God's signs.

---

* The Yiddish name for Brest-Litovsk.

Warming their mouths in whiffs of flickering candlelight,
they've settled down, as if for *shiveh,* on the earth,
and winds are howling: Who will pity them tonight?
and often, like a sword, an icy star darts forth.

From the Bug River—a ferocious blizzard blows,
wiping out every footstep with its lashing snows;
but on menorahs in the *shuls* of Bialystok,
like worn-out fiddles they have hung their exile up.

Itzik Feffer
(1900–1952)

Born in 1900 in Spole, near Kiev, Itzik Feffer started work at age twelve as a compositor. He became a Communist during the revolution, joined the Red Army, and participated in a number of battles. His first poem was published when he was nineteen, and he soon plunged into literary activity, editing the journals Prolit *and* Challenge, *equivalents of the Proletpen publications, and eventually becoming a member of the presidium of the Union of Soviet Writers. He authored many collections, from* Shavings *in 1922 through* Roitarmei-ish *(In the Red Army Way), issued in 1943 by the Proletpen's successor, YKUF, in New York. The same year, with the great actor Solomon Mikhoels, he toured England and the United States, drawing huge anti-Hitler audiences. His final book,* Once More, *appeared in 1948 shortly before his imprisonment. With Markish, Bergelson, Kvitko, Mikhoels, and many other cultural leaders, he was shot on August 12, 1952. Fifteen years later, a large selected edition of his work,* Songs, Ballads, Poems, *was issued in Moscow.*

Shadows of the Warsaw Ghetto
(excerpt)

O Lord of Creation! Here townspeople lived;
they did their day's labor, they sang and they grieved;
they bellowed a curse here, they murmured a blessing;
here merchants made bargains with customers passing;
here people sat knitting; they danced and they screamed;
here babies in cradles were rocked till they dreamed;
here children were clasped in the hug of their mother;
here guests at grand weddings caroused with each other;
here mourners at funerals melted in tears,
then came home determined to challenge the years;
they hammered here, wrought at their pottery, sewed;
they relished the prize and accepted the load
of falling with grace and advancing with woe
in spite of a world that had marked them as foe.

O Lord of Creation! On this spot the Jew
again drew the gold thread his ancestors drew;
he forged the gold chain here; the peacock of gold,
with maidenly eyes that are bliss to behold,
built here in these orchards a favorite nest;
the dream everlasting came here and was blessed.
In fire the nest fell from high overhead;
the thread of the ages—the bright golden thread—
was left dangling limp from a far, sunny beam;
a hut in the forest now houses the dream;
and no one can say where the peacock has gone;
there's nobody left in all Warsaw, not one
to weep for her beauty bereft of its home.
The doorsteps are silent, the cobbles struck dumb.
Here sentences perish before one can speak,
for this is the Ghetto, and here is its street.

My Curse

My curse—may it fall like a fiery hail in your way.
Your luck—may it smash into bits like a vessel of clay.
And may my curse rankle and roast you wherever you range,
until your vile gullet is choked by my grip of revenge.

Accurst be the mother who thrust you alive from her womb.
The grain in your field—may it wilt and forget how to bloom.
Before the red hand of your reaper can sickle it down,
may nothing but dry, naked sticks be the yield of your ground.

And if you attempt to replenish your acres once more,
then once again let this my curse, that explodes through the roar
of children, through shrieks of the ravaged, through wild
    conflagration,
besiege you and carry your shame to the tenth generation!

May heaven grant you and your deathmates no merciful rains;
your swastika, may it be rinsed by the mud from your veins.
Wherever you go, may you trip on an ambushing stone;
may hooves trample you and whatever you thievishly own . . .

May street curs assemble to shit upon you and your shrine.
Henceforth upon you may the smile of a child never shine.
Across your whole earth, row on row, may the mounds fester high.
And may, like your country, the tree at your window soon die.

Wherever your foot tries to go, where it stops, where it veers,
your murderous flesh—may it sink in the rivers of tears
that drop from the eyes of the mothers, from children's sad eyes,
and shroud the whole world like a smothering cloud in the skies.

The hate for your crimes in the ghettos, no more may it snivel,
but be a great sword, crushing you and your hideouts of evil.
On meadows, on cobbles, on streets, may the blood of the Jew
rise up and turn into the flame that annihilates you.

Accurst be your name, and erased may it be from now on
here under the snows of the stars and the stalks of the sun.
Your crew, may they vanish like dust, and your funeral hearse—
may no one and nothing accompany it but my curse!

The Vow

I swear by the horrified stars, by the sun and its rays,
I swear by whatever a plain man can swear by these days.
I swear by the hearts that are seething where battles rage on;
I swear by the sources of joy that the foe has undone;
I swear by the willows that grieve where the Dnieper is flowing;
I swear by my blood, the unrest in my eyes that keeps growing;
—my hate will not slacken, my wrath will not cool in the storm,
until I can feel it—the enemy's blood on my arm.

Should one of my hands be plucked off by the whirlwind of death,
my second has power to throttle the enemy's breath;
and if, in the path of a bullet, my second goes lame,
my great, holy hate has the power to muffle the pain.

As long as my loyal feet go where I tell them to go—
in fire, in water—I'll find him, the murderous foe.
And if the night blows out my eyes, then in blindness my hate

—my sister in battle—will not let me bow to my fate.
The eyes of my heart will, I swear, hunt you down like a beast
till every last vestige of you is forever erased!

This, then, is my oath, which I swear to my fatherland now,
my tribe, my old mother and father; and this is my vow;
and if I prove false to the pledge that so solemnly binds me,
that day let my people's contempt be the swordpoint that finds me!

And if I don't beat back the foe from my sweet, sacred ground
so that not a shred of his ugliness ever is found,
then fixed be my name to the pillory—shame without end,
the ash of my body refused by the planet. Amen!

Ziame Talessin

(1909–   )

Born in Kalinkovitch, Byelorussia, in 1909, Ziame Talessin lived in Moscow for many years and was a regular contributor to Sovietish Heimland, *an influential literary journal. His Soviet collections of verse include* On My Own Ground, In the Bright World, Songs and Poems, *and* On My Responsibility, *along with several books in Russian. With his wife, the great lyric poet Rochel Boimvoll, he was evacuated to Tashkent as the German armies advanced. They later emigrated to Israel, where he published first* Memorial Lament, *followed in 1980 by* Kometz Alef-O.

Thirst

Sand, harsh as salt, on the palate;
ahead of you, fire and smoke.
Where's one to search out some water?
Drier than dust is your throat.

Across there, behind the barbed wire,
back there, where the foe lies entrenched—
the well of sweet coolness is ours,
but they alone drink and are quenched.

I can't say for certain what drove us
to fight—whether hatred or thirst.
We crept toward the well and, exhausted,
against its sweet coolness we burst.

And then! a weird moving asunder
came down like a rock on my brain:
the well of sweet coolness before me
was clogged to the brim with our slain.

Meyer Charatz
(1912–1993)

Meyer Charatz was born in Shuri in 1912, grew up in Markulesh, a Jewish colony near Beltz, Bessarabia, and moved to Czernowicz, Bukovina, in 1934. He began writing poems as a boy but was not published until 1934, making a great public impression with his "Don Quixote." After serving in the Rumanian army, he was among thousands of Jews stripped of their citizenship. At the outset of the Nazi invasion in 1941, he was among the many Yiddish poets who fled to Central Asia, returning in 1945. Shortly after his brother-poets Markish, Kvitko, Hofshtein, Feffer, Broderson, Halkin, and Platner were arrested, Charatz, too, was imprisoned. Granted amnesty seven years later, he contributed hundreds of poems to Sovietish Heimland *and various left-wing journals abroad. But in 1960 he was the target of attacks by several Jewish colleagues, charged with "bourgeois nationalist tendencies." In 1972, he left for Israel, where his work finally achieved book form with such volumes as* In an Alien Paradise *and* Heaven and Earth *(both 1974) and* Green Winter *(1982).* Selected Poems *appeared in Jerusalem in 1983. Three years later, he won the Itzik Manger Award, and continued producing work of a high caliber until his death in 1993.* Full Face, Profile and Behind the Shoulders, *a posthumous collection, was published in Tel Aviv in 1993.*

To the Skies of Israel

Give me, O skies, a bit of space;
I want to sepulcher my mother.
And let the stone that marks her place
flame where the clouds of Israel gather.

"Braine Charatz"—I don't know where
she breathed her last, on what grim path.
I beg a wisp of upper air
from you, from you, on her behalf.

I beg a little soft white cloud
to fashion her a fitting shroud;
and, one by one, let silent stars
stand at her grave like honor guards.

Give me, O skies, a bit of space;
I want to sepulcher my mother.
And let the stone that marks her place
flame where the clouds of Israel gather.

Rochel Boimvoll
(1914–)

Rochel Boimvoll, daughter of a theater family, was born in 1914 in Odessa. Her first book, Children's Poems *(1930), was followed in 1934 by* Pioneers and Poems. *Two years later, she graduated from Moscow University.* Cherry Trees Are Blooming *appeared in 1939, followed by* Poems *in 1940. During World War II she was evacuated to Tashkent, where the first of her many Russian volumes,* The Heart on Guard, *was issued in 1943. The first poem that follows records the trauma of June 22, 1941, the day of Hitler's invasion.* Love, *a new Yiddish collection, was published in 1947.* A Small Comb *(1959) was written in collaboration with her husband, Ziame Talessin. Several of her poems were translated into Russian by Anna Akhmatova, perhaps the greatest Soviet poet. According to the* Soviet Encyclopedia of Literature, *her* Stories for Adults *is among the most significant Yiddish works of the 1960s. With her husband she later emigrated to Israel, settling in Jerusalem in 1971. New books of her Yiddish poetry appeared in 1972, 1977, and 1979.* Poems of Many Years, *a compilation of her Russian verse, was issued in 1976.*

June 22nd

I went outside, I simply shut the door,
not thinking that it would at once be gone
and that the whole house would be there no more,
that with such ease a house can be undone
and emptied each window and each wall,
that all can burn up in one second, all
that made life livable and free from harm
and kept the hands and spirit warm.

I shut the door behind me and went out,
and never was my coming back in doubt;
who'd think the street that led me forth misled
and was to be a bitter road ahead?
I shut the door for just a little while,
bid nobody goodbye, and with a smile

let myself set off to approach the fate
that, lurking in the distance, lay in wait.

I did not know what was to come about,
but now I know it all (or is there more?).
My voice, that was a warbler in my throat,
within my breast is now a lion's roar.

Spring's Table

The final volley of the war
subsides; unblemished rolls the sky;
and grass begins to sprout once more
from the fresh graves where brothers lie.

Time for spring's table to be set!
The pine-trees: what a sumptuous sight—
like giant flasks of wine! and yet
there's one thing left: to feel delight.

The earth prepares her table, rich
with dish-lakes, flowers from end to end,
and fresh-sprung vegetables, and fish;
yet one thing's missing: to attend.

Banqueters come from everywhere,
but many places still are vacant.
Why is the missing one not there?
Why does he spoil our merry-making?

The girl, is she still getting dressed,
and does her love still fix the braids?
Six million gone—and with the rest
those two have long been in their graves.

No matter on whose fate you call,
open and plain the answer slashes:
"We sent out searchers for them all,
but what they found were mounds of ashes."

The world's four corners open wide
like great glass doors; but through the panes
none of the absent can be spied—
only chill winds along the lanes.

Confused, a fat bee flits around;
she dare not try a flower's perfume.
Just now, a spot of blood she found
seemed to her a red poppy bloom.

Survivors

The eight poets of this group lived directly in the path of Hitler's tanks in 1939. Aside from Zeitlin, who accidentally survived by being in New York at the time, all fled east and spent the war years, under a variety of conditions, in the far reaches of the Soviet Union, returning very briefly afterward to their devastated homes haunted by the ghosts of annihilated loved ones and neighbors. No matter how far they ran —to Israel, Canada, or the United States—the Holocaust held them until they died. In a 1991 interview with a young German scholar, Rajzel Zychlinska confessed that she had not enjoyed one night of wholesome sleep in the half-century since her mother, her sister, and her brothers and their children, perished in Hitler's gas chambers along with all the other three thousand Jews of Gambin.

Avrom Zak
(1891–1980)

Born near Grodno on December 15, 1891, Avrom Zak moved to Warsaw in 1919 and joined its Yiddish Literary Society. After the Nazis took Poland he fled to Grodno but was arrested a year later and spent World War II as a laborer in the East. After the war he returned to Poland, settling in Lodz, a cultural center. He moved to Paris in 1948, to Buenos Aires four years later, and to New York in 1959. Under the Wings of Death *(1921) was the first of many volumes of poetry; he was also a prolific translator.* He wrote for The Day *and* The Forward. *A three-volume autobiography appeared between 1954 and 1958. He died on May 2, 1980.*

Out of the Hot Ashes

It's often past belief that only I, that I alone
of all the millions who had come to grief,
that I without a scratch climbed from the vale of bones.
At times I can't imagine it, it's past belief.

Perhaps I too was burned to ash with all the others,
like them, just like the rest of them, my sisters, brothers,
burned up, burned up like Moses' bush, his desert thorn,
and out of the hot ashes I arose newborn.

But how it happened I'm unable to remember—
as if a mother'd given birth to me once more
to cry out for a reckoning to the last ember

for all who died in flames or in the poison chamber,
for every child and mother butchered in this war,
all, all, six million lives to be accounted for.

Rochl Korn
(1898–1982)

Rochl Korn was born in 1898 in Podliski, East Galicia, and studied in Vienna. Her father, a Hebrew poet, died when she was eleven. A year later, she began writing in Polish but turned to Yiddish in 1919; Village was published in 1928. The Polish authorities persecuted and imprisoned her for her anti-Fascist activities. Until 1939 she lived in Premisle, Galicia, then moved to Lvov, which she fled in 1941 before the Nazi troops. She lived in Kiev, Tashkent, and other Soviet cities for a number of years. Most of her family, however, had been wiped out in the Holocaust. Following the war she moved first to Sweden, then to Montreal, Canada, where she remained until her death in 1982, producing increasingly strong collections such as From the Other Side of a Poem *(1962),* The Grace of the Verb *(1968),* On the Edge of a Moment *(1972), and* Bitter Reality *(1977), a book dedicated to the memory of her slaughtered family.*

I'd Like to Stop

Someday I'd like
to stop at a house,
tiptoe close
and feel the wall—
What kind of clay was used for the bricks?
As for the door, what kind of wood?
As for destruction, what kind of god
camped there to see that none would befall?

What kind of swallow under its roof
furnished a straw and earthen nest,
and what kind of angels in human guise
entered its hall as guests?

What kind of holy men bearing water
met them as they came in from the street,

to wash the dust of earthly roadways,
the dust from off their feet?

And what kind of blessing did they leave
the children big and small,
so that Belshetz, Maidanek, Treblinka,
could not harm them all?

From such a dwelling
with whitewashed railing
amid trees and flowerbeds
of blue and gold and flame,
there came
the killer of my brothers,
of my mother.

I'll let my anguish grow
like the hair of Samson ages back,
and turn the millstone of days
around that bloody track.

Till on some night hereafter
when I hear above me the roar
of the murderer's drunken laughter,
I'll rip the hinges from the door
and the house will be so shaken
that night itself will waken
as the tremors travel up
through every pane and brick and nail and board
from the bottom to the top.

Yet I know, I know, my Lord,
that the toppling walls will bury
only me
and my woe.

Nahum Bomze
(1906–1954)

Nahum Bomze (family name Frischwasser) was born in Sasov, Galicia, in 1906, the youngest of ten children. At the outset of World War I the family fled to Nicolsberg, Moravia, returning home in 1918. Bomze studied in German and Polish-Yiddish schools in Lemberg and also learned prayer-shawl weaving, a major Sasov craft. His first book, In the Days of the Week, *appeared in 1929. He soon moved to Warsaw, where* Barefoot Steps *appeared in 1936 and* A Guest at Twilight *three years later. Like many others, he fled east before the Nazis. His collection* Passage *appeared in Soviet-occupied Lemberg in 1941. He served in the Red Army, but was later evacuated, first to Kharkov, then to Kazakstan, where he worked in a Tashkent kindergarten. Returning to Poland in late 1945, he became editorial secretary of the Lodz journal* Yiddish Writings, *but left for New York after three years. There, in 1949, his* Autumn Wedding *was issued. He died in 1954, while preparing Mani-Leib's posthumous volumes for the press.*

Alone

Alone at midnight lying
I whispered into my ear:
"You have done so much dying;
let Death once more appear.

"You'll wait; you'll shrug, unshaken,
and take the saber's blow.
And when the grasses waken,
up from the ground you'll grow."

Aaron Zeitlin
(1898–1973)

Eldest son of the famed Hebrew writer Hillel Zeitlin, Aaron Zeitlin was born in 1898 in Gomel, the Ukraine. His early work includes Shadows on Snow *and* Metatron: An Apocalyptic Poem, *both issued in 1922; several plays, including* Yakov Frank *(1929); and a 1937 novel,* Earth Ablaze. *He was allied with Melech Ravitch, Uri-Zvi Greenberg, and Peretz Markish in the experimentalist Khaliastre group of the early 1920s. In 1939, he was in New York for the premiere of his play* No Man's Land *when the Nazis invaded Poland; his wife, parents, and children perished. He remained in New York, permanently scarred, as the following poem makes clear.* Between Fire and Deliverance *appeared in 1957. A decade later the first of a two-volume edition of his poems was published. He died in New York in 1973, as preparations were being made to celebrate his seventy-fifth birthday.*

I Was Not Privileged

I left betimes, and God protected me
from the catastrophe.
Why did I leave before what was to be?

I was not privileged to take the road of flame
on which my people came.
And it torments me like a sin beyond forgiving,
the guilt of living,
of living on and singing on in rhyme.
And I'll be poisoned by my crime
until I follow one of the three shapes
prepared to shield me from my guilt, each of which waits
and calls me with its glowing word:
Saintliness is the first, Insanity the second,
Suicide the third.

But not by suicide can one so weak as I be beckoned;
my petty nature's not ascetically inclined;
nor have I the capacity to lose my mind.

Binem Heller

(1908–   )

Born in Warsaw in 1908, Binem Heller became a glove worker at four-teen. He emerged early as a leader of Poland's proletarian poets, equiva-lent to the Proletpen, with his first collection, Through the Bars, *published in Lodz in 1930. From 1937 to 1939 he lived in Belgium and Paris. He returned to Warsaw, then fled to Bialystok before the Nazi armies. After the invasion of the Soviet Union he took shelter in Alma-Ata and in 1947 returned to Poland hoping to participate in a revival of its Jewish cultural life.* Spring in Poland *appeared in 1950 and* Poems, 1932–1939, *in 1956. He then moved to Paris and Brussels, where his poem of political renunciation, "Alas, How They Shattered My Life," caused a storm of controversy. A year later he made Israel his home. His many later works include* New Poems *(1964),* It's the Month of Nissan in the Warsaw Ghetto *(1973), and* They Shall Arise *(1984).*

A Song about Yiddish

The Jews are dead; their language is alive.
She also lives when sorrow must be spoken.
And many are her juices that revive.
And she has silences that will be broken.

All in a row some people were marched by,
and in the selfsame row they all were murdered.
They heard no other sound than the raw cry
of German jaws by which their death was ordered.

And when in thousands they stood yellow-starred
beside the graves they had been summoned for,
their mother tongue grew suddenly so hard,
and against all monstrosities—so poor.

For life, it is the living speech we speak;
for death, only the liturgy will do;
in time of death the mother tongue is weak,
and in life only, can she live anew.

The Jews are dead. With ashes and with earth
their mouths have everlastingly been shut.
But once again their mother tongue blooms forth
and does not know that she's been rooted out.

Israel Emiot
(1909–1978)

Israel Emiot (pen name of Israel Goldwasser) was born in 1909 in Ostrau-Mazowietsk, Poland. His father went to America in 1919 to study medicine, but instead worked as a presser and died young. The boy was brought up by his grandparents. He wrote Hebrew verse as a child; when he was seventeen, his work began to be published. Among his early volumes are Drops in the Sea *(1935) and* On the Side *(1938), both published in Warsaw, which he fled before the Nazi troops, returning to his birthplace. A week later, when the Germans shot his mother, he escaped to Bialystok. He began publishing in the Soviet Yiddish press; a new collection,* Poems, *edited by Aaron Kushnirov, appeared in Moscow in 1940. After Hitler's invasion of Russia he was among the many refugees evacuated to Alma-Ata, Kazakstan. He went to Biro-Bidjan in 1944 as a correspondent for the Jewish Anti-Fascist Committee and remained until 1948, when he was incarcerated for a year, then deported to an eastern Siberia camp, where he met Moishe Broderson and other poets. Granted amnesty in 1953, he went to Poland, where his poems were published in Polish, and* Yearning, *a new collection, was issued in 1957. He moved to the United States, where his wife and children had found refuge in 1940, and ultimately settled in Rochester, New York, where* The Biro-Bidjan Affair, *with an introduction by Melech Ravitch, appeared in 1960, followed by* Listening to the Tune *in 1961 and* Covered Mirrors *two years later. He died in 1978.*

Had My Mother Lived

Had my mother lived, by now she'd surely be
an old Jewish woman with hair white as snow;
even through spectacles she would not see
the difference between dream and what is so.

An old, old mother, with nothing left to do,
feet propped on a stool, a princess on her throne;
but whatever you're up to, she'd be right there with you
—and your whole life comes from her alone.

"Momma, the table waits for you," I'd say.
As portraits crown walls, she'd crown each holiday.
And if she drowsed, I'd gently take her hand
and off we'd wander to her golden land.

Mendele

Now the Holocaust's done and there's scarcely a Jew,
I turn, Grandpa Mendele, once more to you.

You visited me as a workaday guest
to shake me, awaken some hope in my breast.

But speak to me, Mendele: do you know why
my Sender has suddenly started to cry?

—O Grandpa, it's lonely and I kiss every word
of Ben Yomen the Last, of Ben Yomen the Third,

who salutes me in Yiddish, and sets me at rest
when walls stick their ears out, as if they're nonplussed.

We heard you, dear Grandpa, and gathered your lore,
and nevertheless remained fools as before.

And I keep, as before, although years have gone past,
the old Jewish custom: hope wakes in my breast.

Chaim Grade
(1910–1982)

Chaim Grade was born in Vilna in 1910. At twenty-two, he began contributing poems to the Vilna Day *and became a member of the progressive group Young Vilna. His first collection,* Yes, *appeared in 1936. This was followed by* Musserniks *three years later. He fled east and spent World War II in the USSR, returning in 1946 to the city of his birth, where his wife and family had been slaughtered with tens of thousands of others. He stayed briefly, trying to reestablish Vilna's once-brilliant cultural life, but left for Paris in 1947 and two years later settled in New York. From 1945 to 1950, six volumes of his poetry appeared—the first,* Epochs, *in New York, the last,* The Radiance of Extinguished Stars, *in Buenos Aires. A dozen years passed before his next collection,* The Man of Fire. *In 1967 his novel,* The Well, *was published in an English translation. Two years later his last book of poems,* On My Way to You, *was issued in Tel Aviv in a Hebrew-Yiddish edition.*

A Naked Boy

Creator of the world in all its diverse forms!
A naked boy comes with a girl-child in his arms.
He holds his sister, since she is the lastborn daughter.
He takes her from Treblinka, from the place of slaughter.
He keeps on moving in the sky above my head
on fields of ice amid the swarms of stars outspread
and in the blazing heat of sunlit mountaintops,
and never wants to get somewhere and never stops.
Around his neck the little sister's hands are clasped
as in the death march to the cell that was their last.

Creator of the tents of Heaven far away,
of our bad world, and of the good worlds in your sway!
The hissing snake that twists itself up into arcs
looks not the slightest bit like your melodious larks;
nobody can transpose the shapes of these two creatures;
but Man hides what he is by altering his features.

The hangman's fingers are as white as are his slain;
and once the hangman dies, he cannot die again.
Only the boy goes on, and carries as he goes
his sister, as the seed bag's held by one who sows.

The twelve old stars of fate have ringed me like barbed wire,
and now the star of this boy's fate. It's my desire
to find his native land, his own beloved town
where he at last can lay his little sister down;
and I have found a simple hill at Galilee
where all the trees will murmur sympathetically.
But even at blue Galilee he will not trust
his sister's cold and naked body to the dust.
And still in moonlight he keeps wandering about
around Treblinka's altar, where the fire is out.

Rajzel Zychlinska

(1910–   )

*Rajzel Zychlinska was born in Gambin, Poland, on July 27, 1910. Her
father, Mordecai, a leather worker, hoped to establish himself in the
United States; but his wife, Deborah, descended from rabbis and Talmu-
dic scholars, held back, reluctant to expose her children to a nonreligious
environment. In 1928, during his third effort at relocation, he died in
Chicago. The same year, his daughter's work first appeared in print.*
Poems, *her first collection, with an introduction by Itzik Manger, was
published by Warsaw's Yiddish PEN Club in 1936. The same year she
moved to the capital city. In 1939, weeks before the Nazi army arrived,
the PEN Club issued her second volume,* The Rain Sings. *With Warsaw
in the grip of Hitler, Zychlinska was among those who saved their lives by
fleeing east. She found shelter in the war-harrowed city of Kazan. Here
she married a fellow refugee she had known in Warsaw, now a Red Army
doctor. Their son was born in 1942.*

*Poland after liberation was unbearable for her: all she had loved were
dead, and anti-Semitism raged against the few survivors who returned.
A 1945 pogrom resulted in scores of Jewish dead. With husband and
child, she moved to Lodz. Here her third volume,* To Clear Shores,
*dedicated to the memory of her slaughtered family, appeared in 1948.
The same year, she migrated again, this time to Paris. Three years later,
she settled in the United States; but for the poet there has never been a
real end to her wanderings—from one end of New York to the other,
from east coast to west, then back, and—for a time—across the border
into Canada. Through it all, well into her eighties, Zychlinska has kept
unwavering faith with her gifts and her ghosts. Three powerful volumes
—*Silent Doors *(1962),* Autumnal Squares *(1969), and* The November
Sun *(1977), along with groups of more recent poems, testify to her ever-
ripening craft and her ever-deepening eloquence as a witness to the Holo-
caust, as the voice of its eradicated millions. Honored with Israel's
prestigious Itzik Manger Award in 1975 and a large Leipzig edition of
her selected poems in German translation six years later, Zychlinska is
widely recognized as an authentic giant of our time, who stands with
Sutzkever as one of the greatest living Yiddish poets.*

The Silent Partner

Three meters wide
six meters deep
and fifteen meters long—
these are the measurements of one of the pits
in Poland
to which the Germans drove Jews
shot them there
and buried them.
Three meters wide
six meters deep
and fifteen meters long—
the three dimensions.
And the fourth dimension,
the one in which all the slaughtered Jews
cannot die
and cannot live—
is now the silent partner
through all the days of my life.

My Mother Looks at Me

My mother looks at me with bloodied
eyes, out of a cloud:
Daughter, bind up my wounds.
Her gray head is bowed.

Amid the leaves of each green tree
my sister moans:
My little daughter, where is she?
Rajzel, gather her bones.

My brother swims in the waters
days, weeks, years,
dragged forward by the rivers,
flung back by the seas.

My neighbor wakes me in the night;
he makes a woeful sound:
Take me down from the gallows—
put me in the ground.

May. With my son in my arms I wander
amid shadows. I greet them all.
So many cut-down lives are clinging
to me, to my concerns, to every wall.

So many cut-down lives are trembling
on the long lashes of my son.
So many cut-down lives are sobbing
in May, when the spring winds come.

This Is Not the Road

This is not the road,
and this is not the city.
                    —2 Kings

And where is the road?
Where is the city?
The sun is ready to go down,
and I have not yet found
the spot
the stone
on which to lean my head for a night's rest
and again see the ladder in my dreams
with the angels
who still deliver me
from the flames.

My Prayer to the Chimney

Every morning I offer a prayer
to the chimney,
the godly fool on my roof:

Lessen the frosts from the north,
tame the sun in the south,
and beg the winds
not to knock you down.
For as long as you stand,
I stand too;
as long as you think,
I think too.
Don't fall,
O don't cave in,
my god!

We Go On Living

We go on living on the earth
that has taken our blood to quench its thirst.
There is a green spring coming—
our bones have been ground up into ash;
we go on living, a cluster left to say Kaddish.

We eat the bread of the wheat fields,
drink from a well these days.
The sun is very kind now;
she touches us with her rays . . .
We pass, leading our children by the hand,
wrecked homes, wrecked walls that mournfully stand.
We pass dead islands of dead childhood years.
Free as a bird the wind careers.

We go on living. The snow begins to fall.
We meet white trees, yes, we see them one and all.
Eyes dark, we drink the dusk; and without words
we speak—to little, gray birds.

A Snow Falls

A snow falls in the dusk
and falls.
Streetlamps stretch forth white hands.
There blunders in the snow in the dusk
a deported
alien
homeless Jew.

The snow falls and falls
not from heaven,
not to earth,
but out of some distant,
bloodless planet—
the Jew will go off
and leave no track,
and will never
again come back.

I Live on the West Side

I live on the West Side,
the sun sets here.
Here at dusk the heavens are ablaze
and the river runs blood.
Whose blood?
The streets whirl intoxicated by the flames.
Whose eyes burn in the flames,
whose hair?
Window-frames flutter long and lorn
in the last glow.
The sun sets—
long shadows accompany me
to my doorsteps.
Whose shadows?
The first star appears in the sky.
Venus?
It's a frozen tear of my people.

Prayer

Earth,
let me drink once more
the scent of your grasses—
With the stirring of the trees
in your forests,
let me swim again
to clear shores.
Let the gray bark of your pine trees
welcome me again.
For all drowns
in a bloody fog.
The leaves scream,
and the sun stabs.

Earth,
let me drink once more
the scent of your grasses.

God Hid His Face

All the roads led to death,
all the roads.
All the winds breathed betrayal,
all the winds.
At all the doorways angry dogs barked,
at all the doorways.
All the waters laughed at us,
all the waters.
All the nights fattened on our dread,
all the nights.
And the heavens were bare and empty—
all the heavens.
God hid his face.

How Cool, How Velvet-Green

How cool, how velvet-green
the moss was in those Polish woods
where amid pine trees
I dreamt in the days of my youth.
How pearl-white were the clouds
in the blue heavens—
the green, plush moss
was only a thin cloak
over the open graves
awaiting me.
The silver clouds—
no more than cataracts
on the blind eyes of God.

Tadzhio! Tadzhio!

Tadzhio! Tadzhio!
a mother called
to her blonde boy
back home one evening—
so many years ago,
but the Polish name,
the soft sound
still falls like dew on my spirit
as it did then,
when I was a child.
Tadzhio, Tadzhio,
blonde, golden Polish boy,
did you too help slaughter Jews?

Dear Neighbors

Buy, buy, dear neighbors,
buy this piece of earth.
Cheap, a great bargain!
You'll build yourselves a house here,
dig a well,
and under the window a garden will bloom.
No ghost will come to haunt your place.
My mother won't return from the gas.
Nor will her grandchildren appear.
Nor will I ever again be here
with my tear.
I only take a stone—
it used to feel my mother's feet.
In foreign, wanderer nights
it may pillow me asleep.

The September Wind

The September wind repeats my brother Yukev's
last request:
Yashek, I'll hide at your place
in the empty shack;
just bring me,
sometimes,
a little water,
a piece of bread,
and I'll survive.
But Yashek, our Polish neighbor, did not answer.
From the trees, with their yellow leaves,
my brother Yukev's final words fall dead.
All the empty shacks in the world
stand now
wide open and wait—
and wait for my dead brother Yukev
to come drink water
and eat bread.

Two Stones

The stream close by our house
began
in the eyes of my brother—
quiet and gray.
Quiet and gray runs the stream;
two stones look at me:
the eyes of my brother—
free now of fear and hope.

My Sister Chaneh

On the green grass,
behind the high hill,
strays Chaneh, my sister.
I call her at night—
Sister mine, come!
She does not reply;
the chestnut trees whisper.

On a cool cloud,
in a blue ship,
swims Chaneh, my sister.
I call her by day—
Sister mine, wait!
She does not reply,
and swims away.

But often the mirror cries.
I peer deep into
the lonely eyes
of Chaneh, my sister.
The hair has gone gray—
no, this is ash,
the white, gray ash
of Chaneh, my sister.

My Mother Sang Me a Polish Song

My mother sang me a Polish song:
In everyone's field the rye is greening,
but of my wheat there's not a sign—
Yashek my beloved comes no longer,
Yashek has stopped coming to me—

My mother sang me the Polish song—
in her eyes was heaven.

My Father's Letters

My father's letters from America
to my mother
always began:
Best of wives Deborah!
And if my mother was the best,
the most beautiful,
why did he run
three times to America?

I know, I know,
Mother was pious,
she did not want to sail to America
and see her children
work there on the Sabbath.
Mother was pious.
And maybe I should sail to Chicago
for an answer?
seek out the cemetery
where my father rests in a grave,
with a monument at his head,
a stone—
and mother?
over the fields of Poland winds have blown
the ashes of her bones.

The *Titanic*

When I was
two years old—
the *Titanic* went down.
My mother rocked me
with the *Titanic*.
"As the *Titanic* went down
on a beautiful bright day,
so went down—"
I don't recall whose life
she lamented,
which had gone down
on a beautiful bright day,
like the *Titanic*.
And maybe even then it was
her own life she lamented,
which afterward went down
in the gas-chambers of Chelmno?

They're looking now for the *Titanic*,
submarines,
divers look for the *Titanic*
in the deeps of oceans—
and if they find the ship
and raise it to the surface
after so many drowned years—
then I too may recall
whose life my mother lamented,
which went down
on a beautiful bright day,
like the *Titanic*.

Sounds from the Past

Sounds from the past
revive in my memory:
a funeral in the village,

a black coffin,
I, a child,
chase after the white, swaddled feet
of a corpse—
all the way to the graveyard.
Such a beautiful tree—
such a young tree—
women wail and weep.
Around them trees murmured,
lofty, green crowns,
and I did not know
which tree they meant.

A wedding in the village—
I push toward the canopy,
I touch the white veil of the bride.
Lamps flicker in the wind—
somebody shouts:
Here comes the groom!
Here comes the groom!
Gangway!
Sounds from the past flicker in my memory,
last sparks from a congregation
of extinguished Jews.

Perhaps

Perhaps
today I see Dr. Mengele
drinking a glass of beer
in Tel Aviv
at the sea—
a pair of blue, sharp eyes
suddenly flashed at me
a cold stare of knives.
A smile, manufactured and fake,
suddenly stirred the horror awake—
left, right, left, right,
left!

To the gas!—
Courteously he introduced himself
to those at the next table:
his ancestors were English, Scots,
and on his mother's side
he is "Deutsch."
I withdrew from the cool terrace
and walked a long time in the heat
at the sea
and heard the billows mockingly repeat:
"Deutsch, Deutsch, Deutsch"—

In California I Heard

In California I heard
the lament of the mourning-dove.
Does she mourn the Destruction of the Temple?
the fate of the Jew?
the days that vanish
never to return?
Does she mourn the fate of the doves
that lie at winter
frozen
on the pavement?
In California,
in the land of flowers and grapes—
I heard the lament
of a dove.

My Son

My son,
how the red shirt adorns you!
As if the flames
from which I barely escaped
wanted to light up your face now
with their reflection.
My son,
how the red shirt adorns you!

What Swims There on the Hudson

What swims there on the Hudson
in the glare of red?
Who screams there—rescue us,
we're going under . . .
These are my own, my dead,
the burned to cinder,
who once more, in my memory,
are going under.

And Always When the Sun Goes Down

And always when the sun goes down,
I see the Christ of Titian.
Last rays fall
on his pale hands
and limbs,
rushed to a grave
before night
and darkness.
And always when the sun goes down,
I see those
who were gassed,
incinerated,
so many pale, unlucky hands,
a forest of hands,
and not one sunray
pitied them,
and no grave was allotted them.

The Eclipse of 1964

Slow and sure,
like God's sword,
the long shadow of the earth
lowered itself
over the moon,
and her face grew dark.

Her spectral premonitions
have been fulfilled—
she is wrapped in the smoke
of burning Jews.

Again I Live

*The sun has gone down,
the boy's disappeared
and Chavele still sits in the forest*
—Z. Schneour

Again I live on the West Side.
I watch the setting of the sun
and sit, long after it is gone,
on a bench.
This is how Chavele once sat
alone in a forest—
the sun went down
the boy disappeared
and Chavele sat alone
in the forest.
In what mattress in Germany
do her gold-blonde curls now rot?
Where, from what chimney
did the boy ascend to heaven
in smoke?
Treblinka?
Auschwitz?
The sun could answer me,
but she's silent.
She's involved
with her own burning.

From Across the Wide Sea

From Across the Wide Sea

It has always puzzled and dismayed me that, for all the wisdom acquired at such a bitter price from the Holocaust experience, some editors—half a century later—still refuse to absorb the most poignant lesson of the Warsaw ghetto: only when a tiny remnant remained did the right-wing, left-wing, and center in Warsaw set aside their fierce lifelong antagonisms and unite in a holy battle for Jewish survival. In the pages that follow, and in this collection as a whole, I have tried to achieve the same unity.

The poets of this final group, though geographically removed, were without exception transformed by the Holocaust. Manger's brother died a refugee in Uzbekistan and all of Daniel-Levitch's maternal kin were annihilated, but *each* poet lost precious family clusters—aunts, uncles, cousins, nephews, nieces—who had not joined the westward migrations and whose existence is now recorded only in faded letters and photos.

Leivick, Glatstein, and Molodowsky, among others, moved from brilliance to greatness as poets of the Holocaust. But they had always chosen Jewish themes. On the other hand, all the Proletpen poets, led by Ber Green, I. E. Ronch, and Yuri Suhl, excluded Jewish content from their work until the Nazi horror unfolded. Only then did they release from memory the vivid images of a shtetl childhood and the magnificent rhetoric of Isaiah and Jeremiah.

All Yiddish poets, from that time until their death, knew that theirs was a holy mission: to use their extirpated language as lusciously and memorably as possible to speak on behalf of the millions whose voice had been muted. No one has expressed this truth more powerfully than Binem Heller, the superb survivor-poet:

> The Jews are dead. With ashes and with earth
> their mouths have everlastingly been shut.
> But once again their mother tongue blooms forth
> and does not know that she's been rooted out.

H. Leivick

(1888–1962)

Leivick Halpern, who took the pseudonym H. Leivick to avoid being confused with another great poet, Moishe Leib Halpern, was born in Igumen, Byelorussia, in 1888. Often arrested for socialist activities from 1906 on, he spent four years in a Moscow prison and in 1912 was sentenced to lifetime exile in Siberia. He escaped, traveled across Europe, and reached America in 1914. Here he became a leading member of Di Yunge, along with Mani-Leib, Zische Landau, and Moishe Leib Halpern. He coedited a literary journal with the great novelist Opatoshu and produced several verse-plays, most notably The Golem *(1921). Years of hard work led to tuberculosis, and he spent three years in a Denver sanatorium. Among his early books are* Under Lock and Key *(1918),* Fallen Snow *(1925), and* Through Seven Deaths *(1926). A* Complete Works *(1914–40) was issued in two volumes. After the Holocaust, he produced a series of extraordinary works, including* I Did Not Go to Treblinka *(1945),* The Wedding at Fernwald *(1949), and* Job's Epoch *(1953).* A Leaf on an Apple-Tree *(1955) was followed four years later by* Songs of the Eternal *and* In the Baths of the Tzar. *He died in New York in 1962.*

My Father Used to Call It Chtsos

Midnight. My father used to call this hour *Chtsos.**
I envy it with a great envy. Fifty years,
letter by letter, everywhere I go it goes:
The Exile of Shekinah, as he chanted it in tears.

I do, it seems, as he did: I exclaim my grief
for ruined villages and for their guiltless slain.
I clamp my mouth shut, like my father, teeth on teeth.
Just one thing's missing: his red beard aflame.

---

* Midnight study and prayer to commemorate the destruction of Jerusalem.

That fiery beard of his has vanished with the wind,
and I've been no more lucky with a beardless face;
the *chtsos*-lament, by which the two of us are twinned,
at last arises in the light of childhood days.

And fifty years from now, will my sons also ache
for me? will they perhaps then yearn with the same yearning?
at night will they too, tremblingly devout, awake
and feel at least a line or two of mine still burning?

If so, O Lord of Time, hear me and grant thy grace:
allow my sons a little mercy, I implore thee:
as chalk is stricken from a slate, wash off, erase
these monstrous nights of mine, the nights of nineteen-forty.

Sara Barkan
(1888–1957)

Sara Barkan was born about 1888 in Dvinsk, Latvia. Her father was a Yiddish teacher and writer. She married a tailor and in 1907 followed him to America with their first child. In 1922, she made her debut as a writer of verse for children. Good Springtime, *her first volume, was published in 1936, followed by* Gifts *a decade later.* Stories and Songs of Every Day for Big and Small *was issued by the YKUF in 1956. A year later she died in her hometown of many years, Maplewood, New Jersey.*

To an Orphan

I hear your lament from across the wide sea;
through smoke and through flame you are staring at me.
When bread's on my table you wait for a crust,
and when I am dressing you quake from the frost.

How can I forget? I *must* recognize you—
when I was a child, I was fatherless too;
in bed I would suck on my fingers—just so;
and once, in a winter, my supper was snow.

I stand here and cut me a slice of fresh bread,
and swear by the sun, by its midsummer red,
that the bite I have taken may stick in my throat
if it isn't your sobbing I hear in the pot!

I bite my lips bitterly—you are my child!
Your eyes make me tremble—they're driving me wild.
You keep me from sleeping, you nudge me awake.
This day—no, this hour! I must act for your sake.

Shifre Weiss
(1889–1955)

Born near Kovno, Lithuania, in 1889, Shifre Weiss was orphaned at twelve when her father, on his way to America, was murdered in a neighboring village. Three years later, she joined the Bund and became a skilled orator. Hunted by the police, she escaped to America in 1905. She lived first in Pittsburgh, then in Chicago, and finally settled in California in 1917. She helped found the Hollywood Workmen's Circle. Her poems and articles appeared in Die Freie Arbeter-Shtimme, Morning Freiheit, Yiddishe Kultur, *etc. Her books include* On the Way *(1932),* To the World *(1943), and* To the Dawning Day *(1953). She died in 1955, while traveling from Los Angeles to Florida.*

Dreams

I am the tablets
of all the dreams I've dreamt.
Wild storms have torn up
my Testament.

My fathers wrote a Torah
that I was proud to shield
as the sun tends May buds
for ripe October's yield.

The hailstones of life
hammered at my panes—
tore up my holy pages,
swept them away in the rains.

I live now to assemble
the alphabet of the ages—
to rescue the dreams I dreamt,
rewrite the holy pages.

Eliezer Greenberg
(1896–1977)

Eliezer Greenberg was born in 1896 in Lipkan, Bessarabia, birthplace of the poets Eliezer Steinbarg, Jacob Sternberg, and Moishe Altman. In 1913, he emigrated to the United States and attended the University of Michigan, ultimately settling in New York in 1927. For some years he contributed to the Morning Freiheit, Hammer, *and* Signal *as well as to the journals of the opposite camp.* Streets and Avenues *appeared in 1928, followed by* From Everywhere *(1934),* Village of Fishermen *(1938), and* The Long Night *(1946). From 1951 to 1954 he served as vice-president of the Yiddish PEN Club. With Irving Howe he later edited anthologies of Yiddish fiction and poetry in English translation, and for several years served as editor of* Tsukunft. *His final collections were* Eternal Thirst *(1968) and* Remembrance *(1974). He died in 1977.*

I. L. Peretz and Bontshe Shvaig in the Warsaw Ghetto

At twilight, when the final rays are shed
of a consumptive sun that's almost dead,
when a limp weariness begins to fall
upon the ghetto-town—a hollowed skull—

when grayer grow the hours as shade falls thicker,
and petrified by dread one's breath comes quicker,
when sunset blossoms red, like bloodstains on a wound,
and yellow as a Torah parchment glows the moon,

out of a somewhere no one knows, down streets
filled with dead silence, comes the sound of feet.
I. L. Peretz creeps by, and in his pallid face
two eyes glow brightly, like two stars ablaze.

The same broadbrimmed black hat of long ago
sits on his lion-head bedecked with snow;
he comes now from a world far, far away—
and looks at his old home in horror and dismay.

Nothing but heaps of ash—and, round about,
are clay and brick; the walls, the buildings lie stretched out,
prayer-house and poor-house, and on all a loneliness,
on all, a desolate distress.

But suddenly a band of Jews plods by
with yellow patches, and with eyes that mutely cry;
from weary heads, oh how much anguish weeps!
on buckling backs, oh what a pack of griefs!

A herd of voiceless kine, they clump ahead,
gaping at Peretz with suspicious dread:
(a man without a yellow patch is not from here!)
till in the jaws of a deep, crazy night they disappear.

He tries to get the riddle solved: the place? the time?
Till in deep sorrow suddenly it comes to mind—
There once were Nomberg, Reisen, Asch—young eagles three;
and what's become of gentle Denison? Where's he? . . .

All of us dreamt a dream here, grand and bold;
all of us forged a chain, a chain of gold;
alone I stand in the grim valley now, where all outdoors
weeps bitterly on the dry bones, and no limb stirs.

What century is this? What land? Is it the reign
of Titus? Egypt, perhaps? or Tophet? Torquemada's Spain?
A mean wind thrusts its claw inside his cape,
and a fat crow caws past his shuddering shape.

He moves ahead toward the city's heart,
the lifelong smithy of his lyric art;
on a great heap of ash, murmuring prayers
with quivering voice, his Bontshe Shvaig appears.

Bontshe knows his creator, runs to him at once
and holds a hand out in mute reverence.
And that which two eyes ask for, two eyes tell;
as always, Bontshe's mute—but night and Peretz hear him well:

Battles, ghettos, lime-kilns, gases, flames unfold,
dread glare of swastikas (and both are feverish with cold!)
Choked sobs, wild cries, a damned inheritance of plagues—
once more the world is burning Jews at all the stakes!

Bontshe proceeds, with Peretz at his heels.
Along an ink-black sky a bit of clear cloud sails
on oceans of disaster; on and on
they go, till Bontshe halts at Ceglana #1.

A single stone is left of the demolished house,
and to that stone, that naked remnant, Bontshe bows;
a sobbing rocks the stillness of the night,
and Peretz hearkens, riven by distress and fright.

Here—Bontshe points—is where you lived and kept the flame!
Here's where you forged the chain, the golden chain!
You also made me here, and are rewarded for my story . . .
The glory you can keep, the whole fireworks of glory!

I want to cry out all my years of keeping still;
I want a tongue from you, I want to speak my fill!
My whole life I said nothing . . . and uncaged, unchained,
even the wild beasts shunned me; I alone remained

to tell how the world hushed, how the Creator hushed
when our whole nation—kith and kin, the rich, the poor—
    were crushed.
My maker, call the world again to Judgment! but this once
let me, forever speechless, speak in their defense!

Allow my lips, forever locked, to open;
after a lifelong silence, let the seal be broken!
Allow my heart, that year by year in secret cried,
bolted by thousand bolts, to open wide! . . .

His lamentation rises and becomes a roar,
and now it rages like a wolf and dove at war;
till morn with feverish madness sets the world ablaze.
And Peretz howls, and Bontshe howls—and the surroundings freeze.

"How lone, how like a widow sits the city once so teeming!
that thrilled the land once like a bride in glory gleaming!"
—Two Jews rock themselves, and a wan moon looks down:
Peretz and Bontshe, one lone pair in all the town.

.   .   .

Until a new day sprouts up in the east:
a saucy sun that's not embarrassed in the least.
And, also unembarrassed, awake and not gone mad,
she found a Yiddish poet—setting down the dream he had.

Kadia Molodowsky
(1894–1975)

Born in 1894 in Bereza Kartuska, Lithuania, Kadia Molodowsky first taught and published in Odessa and Kiev, then became an extraordinary Yiddish schoolteacher in Warsaw, where she was persecuted by the police for her anti-Fascist activities. Her early volumes include Autumn Nights *(1928),* Dzika Street *(1930), and* Small Shoes Go Away *(1933). In 1935 she emigrated to New York, where she produced* Young Jews *(1945) and* King David Remained Alone *(1946). Except for a two-year sojourn in Israel (1950–52), she lived in New York until her death in 1975. Distinguished for her work in drama and fiction, she is best known for several volumes of luminous prophetic poetry, notably* Angels Come to Jerusalem *(1952),* A Room with Seven Windows *(1957), and* Light of a Thorn Tree *(1965), and for her children's verse, collected in* Marzipans *(1970).*

Merciful God

Merciful God,
select some other nation
for a while.
We're sick of dying and the dead.
We have not one more prayer.
Select some other nation
for a while. We have not one more drop
of blood to shed.
Our dwelling has become a desert.
The earth has no space to inter our limbs.
Not one more lamentation's left for us.
The Books contain
not one more woeful hymn.

Merciful God,
make sanctified some other land,
some other mountain.

We have already scattered holy ashes
on all the fields, on every stone.
We've paid for every letter of Your ten commandments
with infants,
youths,
and crones.

Merciful God,
lift up Your radiant brow
and look at other nations—
give them the prophecies and holy days.
In every tongue Your word is babbled—
teach them the Deeds,
the dark ways of temptation.

Merciful God,
give us the simple clothes
that shepherds wear,
or blacksmiths at the hammer,
or washerwomen, pelt-skinners,
the humblest slave.
And grant us one more favor:
Merciful God,
take back the godly genius that You gave.

Jacob Glatstein
(1896–1971)

Born in 1896 in Lublin, Poland, Jacob Glatstein was first published at seventeen. A year later, he settled in New York and, in 1919, turned to Yiddish. The same year he joined N. B. Minkoff and A. Glanz-Leyeles in founding the Introspectivist group of Yiddish writers and their controversial publication, In Zich. *His early volumes include* Poetry *(1921),* Free Verse *(1926), and* Credo *(1929); transformed by the Holocaust, as were most Yiddish poets, his voice deepened in such works as* Songs from Memory *(1943);* My Father's Shadow *(1953),* The Joy of the Yiddish Verb *(1961), and* A Jew from Lublin *(1967). For years he contributed a twice-weekly column, "Plain and Simple," to the* Day-Morning Journal. *Ruth Whitman's translation of his* Selected Poems *was issued in 1966. Two years later he coedited, in English, an* Anthology of Holocaust Literature. *He died in 1971.*

Smoke

Through the stack of a crematory
a puff of Jew goes up to glory;
and just as the smoke thins out of view,
his wife and children go up too.

And in those heavenly upper regions
smoke wisps yearn and weep in legions.
God, where you are thought to dwell,
all of us are not there as well.

Memorial Poem

Eyes of strangers do not see
how I unlock the door in my small room
and my nocturnal walk begins from tomb to tomb.
(How much soil do puffs of smoke require?)
There one passes peaks and vales,

and meandering, hidden trails
enough to last a walker all night long.
In the darkness grave-marks shine
before me with a mournful song.
Graves of the entire
annihilated Jewish world
bloom in this wretched tent of mine.
And I implore:
Be my father, my mother,
my sister, my brother,
the children I've cherished—
be real as a moan,
my own blood and bone;
become my own perished;
let me know the full pain
of six million slain.

At dawn I lock the door
to the graveyard of my people.
I sit at the table
and set myself a-dreaming with a tune.
The enemy did not master them.
Fathers, mothers, babes out of the cradle,
surrounded Death and conquered him.
Astounded, all the little children
ran toward the Death that sought to kill them,
without crying, like lullabied Jewish tales.
And soon each blazed forth into flame
like little carriers of God's name.

Who else has such a private
garden of death at night
as I?
Who else will share my fate?
Whom else does so much charnel-ground await?
When I die,
who will inherit my small cemetery
and the radiant grace
of a memorial candle, bright
with everlasting praise?

Lament for the Souls of Jewish Cities

1.

Souls of Jewish cities,
wrapped in the parchments of eternity.
Will they rise from the valley of death?
Will the breath of life be blown upon them?
Only you, my God, know how powerful they were.
Because you built them with your well-directed might.
But you, my God, knew
how weak they were
before they vanished in smoke.

2.

You did not guard the Jewish cities,
did not fortify them,
so they are like holy letters
chipped off from life.
Voided names now hang
on the doorposts of vacant roads.
All the rims of your world are defiled.

3.

So the souls of Jewish cities
come weeping before God's throne.
God, blessed be He,
see how utterly ravaged we are.
You made us in your image.
Now your world is a piece of flesh,
dumb.
Like pagan bells now ring
the names of cities:
Warsaw, Vilna, Chelm, Lublin.

4.

On the day I build my house,
if I forget the Jewish cities,
may my tongue cleave to the roof of my mouth,
my right hand lose her cunning.

May my tongue, no matter where, cleave to my mouth,
my right hand lose her cunning, the hand
that builds God's house on the mountain
based on so great a forgetting.

5.

In a strayed slumber
the nondreamer and nonsleeper
lets himself recite the perished names
of holy Jewish cities,
sniffs the best flour of their Jewishness.
A charity rises
that is done with all the world.
Thousands of dead children weep hymns of praise.

6.

The People most childlike, most faithful,
with the blood of Jewish cities
in its veins,
in the nightmares
of its hardest exile
has never been frightened
by such horror
as the surrounding world
has brought upon it.
Like a terrified dove
it put forth its neck to the butcher.
Holy, thrice holy,
the frailest child among nations
with the blood of Jewish cities
in its veins.

7.

Without flesh, without bones, only soul,
prophesy, Son of Adam, if you can.
In the valley of slaughter.
That the spirit will also
rise from the ashes mourned in one heap.
Song upon song will be offered up,
smoke upon smoke, longing upon longing,

holiness upon holiness.
And Jewish cities
will rise once more
in the valley of so much
death-louring desolation.
Prophesy, prophesy, prophesy,
till your last breath,
if you can.

Shaye Budin

(1899–   )

Shaye Budin was born in 1899 in the Ukrainian village of Korostitchev. He emigrated to New York in 1915 and remained there. For several years he worked for HIAS. Among his works are Days and Life *(1955),* May My Poems Live *(1969), and* Songs of My Days *(1983).*

What Is Not Here

On sea and on ocean, on night
and on silence, the moon is making her rounds;
she probes in the deep, wakes the soul from its sleep,
and rouses the heart within me.
Rouses my heart and laughs down into my eyes:
Little fellow, what game are you playing with me?

Here is the sky, the sky is here.
Here is the ocean, the ocean's here.
Here is the earth, the earth is here.
And what is not here?

The old man with the long gray beard,
the child in swaddling-clothes,
the girl in the bloom of youth,
the honored name of a family-tree,
the life-to-be in a mother's womb,
the luscious taste of a wife's lips,
the soft-as-velvet glow in a grandmother's eyes.

It is this, that is here no more!

The sky is here,
the ocean's here,
the earth is here.

And what is not here?

The speech of a Yiddish mouth,
the laughter of a loving pair,
the beautiful outcry of I am here,
the happy feeling of honest toil,
the hand outstretched in a friendly greeting,
the love that is eager to be used,
joy at the sight of someone hungry eating.

It is this that is here no more!

The sky is here,
the ocean's here,
the earth is here,
and what is not here?

The grandfathers who bore their heritage upon their faces,
the uncles who lived with the Ten Commandments in their hearts,
the fathers who learned "Ein Yankov" and rode to market-places,
the mothers who sang "God of Abraham" and baked challas, nut-
    cakes and tarts.

It is this that is here no more!

The sky is here,
the ocean's here,
the earth is here,
and what is not here?

The bright and spotless room,
Sir Chimney-Sweep with his broom,
the well-kept Jewish quarter,
the water-carrier, with horse and pail,
the gay memorial parties at the shoemakers' house of prayer,
the tailor's prayer-house, with its ovens warming the air.

It is this, that is here no more!

The sky is here,
the ocean's here,
the earth is here,
and what is not here?

The synagogue and the wedding-place,
the groom, and the bride with a veil on her face,
the bride's folks, and the bridegroom's folks,
and Shimmele the wedding-jester, with his jokes.
The meat-market, the butcher who drowses over his wares,
the baskets of bread, the sacks of cucumbers and cabbages,
the wagons full of apples, grapes and pears.

It is this, that is here no more!

The sky is here,
the ocean's here,
the earth is here,
and what is not here?

The letter: simple, not too long; that beloved little song:
Best regards, best of luck,
best of health, and let us hear from you!

Isaac E. Ronch

(1899–1985)

Born in Konin, Poland, in 1899, Isaac E. Ronch lived in Lodz from 1906 to 1913, when he emigrated to the United States. He was sixteen when his first poem was published. In Chicago he attended Northwestern University, taught in the Yiddish schools, had Winds *published in 1923, and coedited* Young Chicago. *In 1924 he settled in New York, where he became a leader in the Proletpen movement, coediting* Signal. *During the 1930s he edited* Proletarian Upbringing, *coordinated a Yiddish Writers Project for the WPA, and wrote several volumes of poetry, including* Indian Summer *(1930) and* Hungry Hands *(1936). His* Selected Poems *were issued in English translation in 1961, as was* In the Desert *a decade later. By then he had made Los Angeles his home, writing prolifically until his death in 1985. His final work,* Praise and Thanks, *a bilingual collection, appeared in 1981.*

The Last One, the First One

1.

Heads bowed low in sympathy,
ghosts are gliding sadly to and fro,
whispering their soundless words at me:
"You're the last—no other shall there be—
last of Jews—you've ripped your clothes in woe."

Time can never soothe my pain.
Not the summer's last unfaded rose,
nor the last chrysanthemum, that snows
cover—but the gentle, pious Jews
shall not ever come to me again.

Like the leaves their lives were trampled under; like
the leaves their ashes deck the lands.
Yet they follow everywhere I wander;
like a wall their grief before me stands;
from the ground they're stretching forth their hands.

2.

Looking out, I search, and ask the air:
"Can I be the last of all the Jews?"
People pass me quickly; everywhere
crowds are pointing to the latest news;
but they do not feel my great despair.

Off I go—the road I take is long—
off to distant fields; and, passing through,
listen to the stalks' unbending song.
Tell me, ageless mother-earth, are you
also sorry for the lone, last Jew?

Mightily the ocean roars,
booms its rage, and beats the shores,
unrest breathing from its face . . .
Waves, oh waves, that wildly chase,
tell me, is my tribe to be no more?

Miles of forest, ranked in regiments;
giant trees, like sentries—overhead
clouds of woe are hanging, black and dense;
you protected sons and daughters once;
you can tell the world who struck them dead.

Mountains crown themselves with peaks of white.
And the vales are endlessly in flower.
Thunder crashes, lightning blinds the sight.
Everything that lives must gather power
for the reckoning, the judgment hour.

I approach the towering rocks, and say:
"Can it be that one last Jew may live
in the crevices—one fugitive
from the camp, who somehow got away
on that day, that death-demented day . . . ?"

3.

On I go, and knock at every door;
whimper, cry aloud, beseech;

search the water for a solid shore;
see the dangers looming . . . more and more . . .
till I'm flung upon a beach.

Flung—upon an isle, a wondrous isle!
Am I dreaming, or am I awake?
Loving eyes embrace me; faces smile;
hands are held out for my hand to take.
Here my wealth was, waiting all the while.

I, the last of Jews, am but the first.
People of the Book of Books am I.
No; my tribe could never be dispersed:
its Commandments blaze across the sky.
Quickly, quickly, let them be rehearsed:

"Thou shalt not kill, nor enslave another!
Thou shalt never take thy neighbor's wife!
Thou shalt not deal falsely with thy brother!
Show respect to father and to mother!
Lead a pure, an honorable life!

4.

From my tribe the first of Bibles came,
first of psalms—with pride I make my claim.
In the prayer-house, glowing with life's flame,
Grandfather once said his prayers, and hurled
scorn upon the evils of the world;
and his jeers put even Death to shame.

Of his children only ash remains;
and their skulls are in the garbage-pile.
Moses, though, who burst his people's chains,
facing Death with a defiant smile—
Moses lives—his fire is in my veins.

Through me prophets' blood forever pours;
Micah shouts in me, and Deborah sings;
in my soul the word of David rings.

When the terrifying blizzard roars
swift Isaiah comes and reassures.

5.

See! the Maccabean lights still blaze,
setting hearts aglow with zeal and trust;
still the wheel turns, bringing joyous days.
Each year Mordecai receives new praise;
every year a Haman bites the dust.

Who can count the heroes I have sung?
Every land has tasted of my dead;
turned my limbs to ash—cut out my tongue.
But, in spite of all the nets they flung,
my Hirsch Leckerts would not be misled.

I'm the burning bush, the desert thorn,
flame that winds can never batter down.
After every death I rise newborn;
my inheritance—a weight of scorn—
till my tears shall sink into the ground.

Last of Jews is still the first to speak—
wakes the world to light, and bears its sorrow;
stands alone and whole battalions quake;
soars up like the swallow of tomorrow;
plants his flag of freedom on the peak.

Homecoming

I am returning from the vale of tears.
I am not what I was in other years.
Death's shadow followed me along the way,
and everywhere men's bones were on display.
I am returning, prematurely gray.

My eyes, that once could burn, no longer burn—
the friends I loved shall nevermore return;
I cannot find them now, and never will:
I call, and no one answers—all is still.
I hear my own voice thrown from hill to hill.

The world was meant to be a lovebirds' nest,
but it's been stricken by a plague, a pest.
The dreams I built were beautiful and sweet;
I shared them with the people on my street—
now Death has crushed them all beneath his feet.

How rare it was to hear a robin sing!
How lovely was the murmur of a spring!
I am returning from the vale of tears.
The voice of woe has sounded in my ears.
I am not what I was in other years.

Ber Green

(1901–1989)

Born in Yaruga, Podolia, in 1901, Ber Green (pseudonym of Itzik Greenberg) was orphaned at infancy. His first poems were in Hebrew and Russian; at thirteen he achieved publication. After experiencing the pogroms and the civil war in the Ukraine, he taught in Rumania (1921–23). Settling in New York in 1923, he became a shop worker, then a Yiddish schoolteacher. He turned to Yiddish poetry in 1924; from that time he was an indispensable participant in every left-wing Yiddish publication and literary group, a tireless creative force as organizer, editor, lecturer, critic, poet, and translator. For half a century (1931–81) he coedited the Morning Freiheit. Flowers under Snow, *his first collection, was issued in 1939. A compilation of critical essays,* Yiddish Poets in America, *appeared in 1963.* Forever Green, *his second volume of poems, was published in Warsaw three years later. He died a few years after the interview with which I conclude this book.*

The Stone

It suddenly opened a mouth, and cried
so that all who heard were horrified:

"Of many friends I stand alone,
a gray old solitary stone.
I was part of a house in days gone by—
but now a remembrance, a symbol am I.

"I, the charred stone, hard and cold,
am a heart grown mute with the grief it holds.
I'm the loneliness of a slaughtered street:
I've watched men rise, and fall in defeat . . .

"Just as a life can be lived in one minute,
a stone can contain a whole city within it.
I was a city of living Jews
laboring, shopping, discussing the news.

"I used to be . . .
But what's become of me?
The sunlit, singing neighborhood
is now a soundless shriek to God.

"The town whose loveliness had shone
like seven suns, became a stone:
silent as children watching in dread,
silent as fathers and mothers dead.

"I am silent, but I speak of a devastating year:
I am one great frozen Jewish tear.
—But I was not idle in the holy fight:
with my sharp edge I shielded and pointed toward the light.

 "When skulls of Nazis were split in two,
I cried: 'Kill them, heroes, while there is breath in you!'
I was barricade for some, and weapon for others,
and I cried: 'You are deathless, sisters and brothers!'

"I ask myself as I stand alone,
a solitary stone:
Do you really know what you are?
A witness of nights that showed no star,
a token of pillage and overthrow,
a weapon of heroes against the foe,
and a fountain of glittering Jewish tears.
You're more than a stone—far more than appears!"

The mouth shut. Silently it stands,
and its silence horrifies the lands.

The Martyrs Are Calling

The village ruined, its people dead;
the synagogue empty, its prayers unsaid.

Where are the grandparents, sisters and brothers, the children safe
    amid dreams?

Dead, brothers, dead they lie in meadows and streams.
Where are the shoemakers, tailors, tinsmiths, capmakers, teachers,
the bathhousekeepers, locksmiths, beggars, cantors, preachers?

Where is the inn, the bathhouse, the reading hall, the mill?
A hill of ashes, brothers, a skeleton-hill.
Over the holy graveyard I wander all alone;
my footstep quakes, my body becomes one heavy moan.

A door, a hinge, a picture-frame,
signs of a life that went up in flame.
A broken gate, a piece of wall—
the sands, the boards . . . grief fills them all.

I search through the wreckage of a home
and find a button, a shoe, a comb,
a rusty knife, a tattered boot,
and a Yiddish letter soiled by the brute.

Across the graveyard like a driven ghost I tread
where bayonets grew drunk and slaughter rioted;
I want to shriek, to roar, but on my tongue the word is dead.

And let us tell the might of—who can tell
of the heroes who hid in caves, of the martyrs who fell?
Some in fire—the unholy ones hurled babes into the flames
before their mothers' unbelieving screams.
Some in water—Don't you hear the rivers, how they thunder
with heroes drowned, with martyrs whom the tides dragged under?

And once again God's earth grows green
on the same spot where mother, child were slain.
Lush fields of cabbage and high grass arise
on the same spot where a whole city lies.
And quietly a little river flows
on the same spot where Jewish streets once rose.

And the sun shines, and leaves adorn the trees,
and the ashes are borne upon the wings of the breeze.
And everywhere wild plants take root—
and the God of Mercy is mute.

And suddenly there lifts a bitter moan
from every smoke-charred stone.
Within the holy ruins a rumbling comes alive:
"World, we shall yet arrive, we shall arrive!"

And suddenly the synagogue is filled with Jews, dead Jews at prayer:
swaying, wrapped in the white shawls they used to wear.
The holy congregation has risen at one word—
and your voice, too, my grandfather, is heard.

In the dark light of candles the ancient prayer-house gleams;
it trembles with the passion of a hundred holy screams.
And suddenly the whole earth's ripped asunder—
the skies turn black, as if with brewing thunder.

The sacred horn of the slain lamb rings out
a sob, a warning, and a wrathful shout:
over mountains of bodies and valleys of bones,
over ravaged market-places, and outraged cobblestones.

through slaughter-fields, and graveyard-neighborhoods,
through inferno-ghettos and partisan woods—
every hamlet, every little town
an altar on which grandfathers and schoolchums were cut down.

Through smoke and fire the shofar-call is hurled,
straining to reach its voice across the world.
Over grave-filled lands the notes are borne,
over corpse-filled meadows of fresh corn:

Repent, indifferent and stone-hearted ones!
Bow down at the ashes of six million daughters and sons!
Beneath ten layers of ash, bury your face:
then wash yourself, be cleansed of your disgrace!

Be cleansed at last, wash off the shame!
The martyrs' blood—can you not hear its scream?
Still unextinguished is Treblinka's flame . . .

World, wipe out forever the unholy one!
His memory begone, his name begone!
Remember: the spirit of revenge lives on.

And the notes console and cry:
Maidanek must not cause your dream to die.
Here where these ash-heaped ruins lie
there'll be a new birth to amaze the sky.

Long life to life! To death with death!
Into the dry bones is blown new breath.

Make strong, my tribe, your body and your soul!
Make yourself whole—a new life's to be charted,
oh partisans, oh Maccabean-hearted!

Itzik Manger
(1901–1969)

*Itzik Manger was born in Czernowicz, Rumania, in 1901. He began
writing Yiddish verse at seventeen and was published for the first time in
1921 in Eliezer Steinbarg's journal* The Awakener. *In 1929 he edited a
journal of his own,* With Measured Words, *and saw the publication of
his first collection,* Stars on the Roof. *This was followed by* Songs of the
Pentateuch *(1935), among other volumes. When Hitler took Poland,
Manger escaped—first to Paris, then to London, where he lived from
1940 to 1951. There, in 1949, he issued a memorial volume for his
brother Noteh, who had perished in Uzbekistan during the war (see the
lullaby "Noteh's Sleep-Song"). * Midrach Itzik *appeared in Paris in 1951.
The same year Manger settled in New York, where* Songs *and* Ballads
*was published in 1952. He made Israel his final home in 1967, and died
there two years later.*

The "Lovers of Israel"

*(An imaginary meeting of three Galician rabbis,
so loved for their wisdom and kindness,
that they were given the name "Lovers of Israel")*

Reb Moishe Leib of Sossow notes the heaps of ash
(the storm has just this instant barreled through);
his beard shakes, embittered are spirit and flesh:
"Come, take a good look, God of Israel, do!"

Reb Wolf of Zborosh murmurs: "Hear, gentlemen, hear!"
(His voice, an evening fiddle, has a weary sound.)
"The Lord of Heaven failed to give His vineyard care.
—A sign: these heaps of ash strewn on the ground."

Reb Maierl of Przemyslan, leaning on his old cane,
stands and waits, delicate but aflame.
"Gentlemen, let us cry out together:

"Creator of the worlds, you are mighty, awesome and great;
but we, the Galicians, erase you from the slate
of the true 'Lovers of Israel' forever and ever."

Nathan D. Korman
(1901–1981)

Nathan D. Korman was born in Rodem, Poland, in 1901. At first a Poale-Zionist, he migrated to Havana in 1926. There his slender volume On Island Earth, *appeared. It was the first Yiddish book of verse ever produced in Cuba. A year later he settled in Philadelphia and worked for decades at the milliner's trade. His works include* Uphill *(1943) and* Days and Years *(1970). He died in 1981.*

The Devils' Dance

Heine goes up in flame, and the Gomorrah;
Spinoza burns, the Rambam and Karl Marx;
around the bonfire Hitler's bullies roar a
devils' dance and hop around the sparks.

Scrolls go up in flame, the holiest pages;
every letter burns, and every line—
all things sacred, treasures of the ages,
are defiled, are plundered from their shrine.

Letters scream into a flaming word:
"Dance, and dance! the final devils' reel!
There'll be no Fourth Reich following the Third;
and every wounded scroll will heal . . . !"

Books laugh as the vandals romp around;
each reads aloud the text that is its own . . .
But though the whole world hears the crackling sound,
men bury in their breasts the bitter moan . . .

Round and round the Nazi ruffians whirl;
with drunkards' nerve they dance around the flame;
it gobbles up and guzzles down the world—
and after? Afterward let ash remain . . .

Heine goes up in flame, and the Gomorrah;
Spinoza, Marx, the Rambam—torn from shelves;
around the bonfire Hitler's dancers roar a
devils' curse—but only curse themselves.

Chaneh Safran
(1902–1994)

Chaneh Safran was born in Schedlitz, Poland, in 1902. Her father ran a small butcher shop. Under the guidance of a wise and culturally oriented mother, she turned to writing at an early age, showing a special gift for drama. In 1916, at the age of fourteen, she left Poland and settled in New York. Her first collection of poems, Victory, *appeared in 1946. This was followed by a second volume,* Today, *and three novels.* Life Calls, *her third book of poems, was issued in 1968. She moved to Florida, where she died in 1994.*

In Terrible Days

My singing was born during terrible days—
on broken, on blood-splattered ways.
Protected from flames were my home and my street then;
I therefore went marching to meet them.

I heard through the air the combined lamentation
of man and of earth in oppression;
I drank from the sea of the sorrows of others
the griefs that imprisoned my brothers.

I wrestled dejection with all my young might
—as fiercely as day wrestles night.
The faith in my heart did not wither away—
no matter how bitter the fray.

This faith was my dower; it came to me through
my father, that virtuous Jew;
within him the strength of his fathers ran strong;
like wine, it fermented my song.

Through me the despair of the wronged found its word,
the courage of heroes was heard;

233

my blood seethed with battle—revenge was its roar;
my world I created in war.

There clamored through me the afflictions of mothers,
of lost little sisters and brothers;
I cheered for the peoples who fought back and won,
who can't be and won't be undone.

Oh I am the mourner, and I am the heir:
man's holiness lies in my care!
With trembling, my song to its sources I tie
and lift the great legacy high!

Yuri Suhl

(1908–1986)

Yuri Suhl was born in Pedayetz, Galicia, in 1908. At fifteen, he came to the United States and settled in Brooklyn. He graduated from the Jewish Workers University in 1932 and began teaching in the Yiddish schools of New York. Inspired by his teacher Ber Green, he soon developed into one of the outstanding Proletpen poets. His first collection, The Light on My Street *(1935), was followed three years later by* Toward the Day *and, in 1942,* Israel Partisan, *a tribute to the anti-Hitler resistance. After serving in the U.S. Army during World War II he turned to English prose, producing two enormously successful autobiographical novels. His documentary volume,* They Fought Back: The Story of Jewish Resistance in Nazi Europe *(1967), remains a classic of Holocaust literature. He also produced many prize-winning children's books. He returned to Yiddish poetry some years before his death in 1986.*

The Ship

1.

This story the billows will tell the sea,
and even the stars will know:
Under cover of night a ship went forth,
and it carried a cargo of priceless worth—
a cargo of human woe.

A load from Oswieczim, a load from Lublin,
a load from Maidanek, a load from Berlin,
a load from Dachau, a load from Treblinka . . .
A ship—such a ship—who would dare sink her?

The motors are roaring,
the ship rides free.
Her grief and her joy
as deep as the sea.

The ship is asail
on the steam of a dream.
Far off the horizon
beckons and gleams.

The shore's coming toward them;
it's close and it's clear.
Hearts pound like hammers;
the hour draws near.

The sea has not ever
beheld such a sight
as the cargo that rides
on the waves tonight.

But suddenly—look at the billows! they burn:
the darkness is riven by luminous rays;
as though by some witchcraft the flood has been turned
into a blinding blaze.

Now sirens are screaming, projector lights glare.
Who are they that suddenly rip
the slumbering Mediterranean air?
Who dares to attack such a ship?

His Majesty's favorite heralds are these,
who'll bugle the ship to shore—
Sir Bevin can't sleep till the refugees
are richly provided for.

He follows their flight with a fatherly eye,
like a mother watching her babes;
and hears every scream, every groan, every sigh
from his window far over the waves.

He's sending a fleet of destroyers en masse
to bring them a merited prize.
He knows how they're yearning for poison gas,
how they're yearning for tears in their eyes.

2.

And those in whose eyes
the tears had stopped
began once more to weep,

and those from whose limbs
the strength had dropped
like giants arose from sleep.

And far out from land
in the middle of night
a battle began
like a blazing light.

3.

The ship is wounded—
she's scarcely astir.
No steam of a dream
is carrying her.

The ship is now borne
on the steam of her woes:
on the steam of a bloody,
blind nightmare she goes.

The blaze has put out
her fiery dream;
no shore—a mirage
beckoned and gleamed . . .

This story the billows will tell the sea,
and the stars—they will hear and turn pale.
Yes, over and over, again and again—
till the whole world rings with the tale.

Chaim Plotkin

(1910–1996)

*Born in Ruzhan, Poland, in 1910, Chaim Plotkin became an apprentice
tailor and a member of the Poale-Zionist movement. Emigrating to the
United States at seventeen, he worked in various clothing factories. In
1929 he published for the first time. From 1930 his work appeared in all
the Proletpen and YKUF publications, including* Zamlungen, *which he
helped establish.* Basic Training *recorded his army service in World War
II. A second collection of his poems,* Along My Paths, *was issued in Tel
Aviv in 1978. He died in 1996.*

Ash on the Sun

The numbers on her arm—
nails of the beast!

She sits at my table
but her soul—*there* . . .

The breath of her talk—
sparks from the smokestacks!

The flames of the ovens
split rocks

and God—
as if eyeless and earless—

her nearest and dearest—
ash on the sun

and the moon—a scythe
weary of slashing!

An hour in a day—
a mountain on her head! . . .

The hands of the ghetto clocks
circle in blood . . .

Her tearless weeping—
a downpour from the heart

.   .   .

I hear and am silent:
I seek word-bandages!

She bears grudges, resents her rescuer
the miracle . . .

Jacob Daniel-Levitz
(1912–1997)

Born in 1912 to the rabbinical Danielevitch family in Kolno, near the German border, the young poet emigrated to the United States in 1929, attended Wayne University, earned a doctorate in sociology from Dropsie College, and taught at the New School for Social Research and Touro College. Under the slightly altered name of Daniel-Levitz his work appeared in Die Freie Arbeter-Shtimme, Tsukunft, *and* Der Veker, *and he translated Ansky's* Dybbuk *into English for Sidney Lumet. The entire maternal side of his family, including his mother, were wiped out during the Holocaust. He died in 1997.*

I Await You

As a pious Jew
awaits Messiah,
I never stop waiting
your safe return
from there, where your grim fate
flung you.
Today, tomorrow
—this is my faith—
I'll get a letter,
a message,
a report that you're alive,
that you're on your way,
And my home
will be filled
with sobs,
with astonishment,
with radiant joy.
Till the last second
of my life,
I will not stop believing
that soon—very soon—
you'll come back.

Because what sense
does life have,
life without you?

Momma

As a leaf tears itself from a tree,
so did I, in a wintry twilight,
tear myself from your home, Momma.

Silvery, a light snow fell
and you, with tear-drained eyes,
came with me to the sleigh:
"Ride off, my child, the world is vast and wide
and open," and your murmured blessing, like a charm
accompanied me on my way.

Many winters have blown past
and though the world has changed so frighteningly
        since that day
and the hand hungry to slay
seized you too as its prey . . .
still glows the snowy twilight
and, Momma, you in tears at the departing sleigh.

Dora Teitelboim
(1914–1992)

Dora Teitelboim, daughter of a house painter, was born in Brest-Litovsk, Poland, in 1914. By the age of twelve she was writing verse. In 1932, she left home for the United States, where she worked several years as a milliner while going to school at night. She became active in both the labor movement and progressive Jewish cultural circles. She also began teaching briefly in Yiddish schools. In 1940, she wrote for the Morning Freiheit, Yiddishe Kultur, *and* Nai-Lebn. *Her poems began to appear in periodicals around the world. Her first volume,* In the Heart of the World, *was published by the New York YKUF in 1944.* Heaven and Earth *followed four years later. The Argentine YKUF issued* With Open Eyes *in 1955.* Facing Life *(1952) and* The Ballad of Little Rock *(1959) were published in Paris, to which she moved in 1960.* Toward Being Human *appeared in Warsaw five years later. For many years, she divided her residence between France and Israel, and was in Tel Aviv when her later collections appeared, including* Song of the Quicksand Generation *(1973),* At the Gateway of Days *(1979),* Before Dawn *(1985), and* Steps to Heights *(1991). Several of her collections were translated into French by Charles Dobzynski and Ratimir Pavlovic. In addition, her poetry has been translated into Hebrew, Russian, Vietnamese, Chinese, and Polish. She died in Tel Aviv in July 1992.* All My Yesterdays Were Steps, *a posthumous selected edition, which I translated, appeared in 1996.*

There Once Was a House

There once was a house on the butchers' street:
an old-fashioned house half-sunk in mud.
They'd a water-barrel for midsummer's heat;
in winter the samovar thawed their blood.

There once was a house that shook with the din
of Jewish singing and laughing and weeping.
Many a midnight the rain poured in
and shared the cradles where infants were sleeping.

There once was a house with a cellar, an attic,
with shutters, a porch; when Passover neared,
the smell of fried goose made them ecstatic;
Fridays they sniffed at the roast, and cheered.

Beside this house was a deep, round well
the whole street drew from. Once in a while
they wrangled and cursed—but after a spell
got over the grouch and managed to smile.

There once was a house whose girls and boys
had bare little feet and clothes that were frayed.
There was never an end to the joys and the noise
that Moisheles, Chaneles, Yoseles made.

At one of the windows a child would perch
and gaze through the pane with a dreamer's eye:
Way past the synagogue, way past the church,
green meadows sprawled, and the Bug flowed by.

If someone was having a difficult labor,
the whole street turned into sisters and brothers:
some brought a tear to comfort their neighbor;
her washing and cooking were seen to by others.

If a holiday came, or a bit of good news,
all rushed around as busy as elves—
some of them patching up old pairs of shoes,
others creating new clothes for themselves.

When Passover-time was in the air,
wealthy and poor stripped every bed.
They scrubbed a year from table and chair,
and out in the sun the wash was spread.

No child skipped off that afternoon:
the courtyard blossomed with bric-a-brac,
and—busily humming a children's tune—
they went through sack after raggedy sack.

A button, a nail, a burnt-out wick,
a smallbox, a key, a rusty chain,
a clock that had long forgotten to tick—
in the eyes of a child they were pirate's gain.

At night the whole house glowed like a bride:
children and grown-ups in holiday dress.
A fragrance of dumplings wafted outside;
the windows ablaze with happiness.

If a stranger blundered to somebody's door,
they cried: Come in and get washed, good man!
Are spoons, forks lacking because we are poor?
Add water—the pot soon boils again!

If someone had no wine for his feast,
he didn't banish the holiday.
He could grace his table with beet-juice at least,
and think the Lord had planned it that way.

Everyone practiced the Passover rite:
some with good wine, with fish and meat,
some with black coffee and matzohs that night
at old wooden tables on wobbly feet.

When Passover came, the house ran on wheels.
All spoke of miracles. Someone confessed
the soup melted dumplings at one of her meals.
There was talk of a Christian disguised as a guest.

But Faivel the Butcher's marvel was greater
than any they'd heard in many a year:
Elijah had come to the pious man's seder
and emptied the goblet and disappeared!

The women dished out this miraculous news
on plates that went clattering far and wide.
The synagogue-yard was astir with Jews
who echoed the tale till the last star died.

It traveled on trains through village and farm.
Some listened and smiled a mischievous smile;
some swore: My beard—may it come to harm!
and trusted the legend for quite a while.

Who knows what would be the end of that wonder;
who knows what oaths they still might take—
had Sarah not spoken one night in her slumber
and Zavel not happened to be awake.

For years that impish wife had been itching
to know the taste of authentic wine.
Too many seders she'd spent in her kitchen
settling for beet-juice . . . But not this time!

The butcher had plenty of wine on his shelf;
of fish and of meat he'd enough and more.
So she made an Elijah of herself,
and watched for her neighbor to open his door.

Now Zavel listened, half-hiding a grin,
and gazed at the radiant face of his mate:
Such nerve! such a madcap, impossible whim!
—but truly he deemed the joke first-rate.

This man was a prayer-clown. From boyhood years
mischief had been his favorite habit;
Father had frequently boxed his ears
for pelting the river with rocks on a Sabbath,

for putting specs on the kitten's eyes,
for wearing the wig of Rebbe's wife,
for tripping old Heinech, for pasting flies
on Rebbe's pointer . . . Ah, that was the life!

Now here was a new bit of mischief to do
to shake up the rich, to shock the devout:
next morning everybody knew
how the butcher's "wonder" had come about.

Such outbursts of fury! such lightning and thunder!
But soon they forgot the whole affair.
Men hoped once more for a holy wonder;
wives sat on porches sunning their hair.

There came a betrothal or other occasion—
a wedding, a "bris"—they embraced on the street;
people poured out for the celebration
and polished the dance-floor with swollen feet.

Yankel would come on such a day:
Yankel the Minstrel, with fiddle and bow.
Sick Bluhme, his mother, had passed away
before he was old enough to know.

Yankel and Poverty were twinborn.
Embarrassed, he would shear his days.
His face was brighter than fresh-ground corn;
eighteen Aprils bloomed in his gaze.

At dawn his melody skipped beside
the kids who were off to Hebrew class.
He played while his empty stomach cried,
till day deserted his window-glass.

Wearing his cap in a cockeyed way—
that cap from which he refused to part;
and the fiddle grandpa had taught him to play—
his loved one, the fiddle—held to his heart.

He played quadrilles at every party
to pull the old folk from their seat,
polkas for the young and hearty,
and even a "freilachs" for a treat.

Yankel would play with soul, with feeling,
till mother-hearts could stand no more.
On top of the table old Nissen went reeling,
while others pounded their boots on the floor.

The girls—like shadows—whirled in a ring
and gazed at the fiddler across the room.
Each secretly prayed that God might bring
a fellow like Yankel to be her groom.

When a string of the fiddle suddenly tore,
it shut up—like a butchered bird.
Then, with one voice, the men would roar,
and the shrill shrieks of wives were heard:

"Play, Yankel, play!
Like your grandpa!" they would scream.
"Stamp, people, while we may!
life is nothing but a dream!"

The boy played tune after tune for them
till the exhausted fell like flies;
and still—with bleary, weary eyes—
whiningly they called to him:

"Play, Yankel, play!
. . . a lively one, a 'freilachs'!"

.   .   .

There once was a house, but it stands no more.
The earth and the sky are just as before.
But the house and the Jews are there no more.

There once was a house with girls, with boys,
with laughter, with songs that may echo yet.
What's left of the children?—a cradle, some toys.
Their names?—the letters of the alphabet.

Of Yankel nothing remains but his cap.
The house is a heap—its floors burnt black.
But deep in the cellar, day after day,
his fiddle waits for someone to play.

Aaron Kramer and Ber Green

Around 1932, my father confronted a remarkably tolerant Ber Green with samplings of my work and asked whether his ten-year-old son had the makings of a poet. Exactly half a century later, in June 1982, I confronted a still-tolerant Ber Green at his bedside in the Home of the Sages, on Manhattan's Delancey Street, and interviewed the ailing belletrist for six hours. One brief segment of our conversation deserves to conclude this book.

June 22 (second meeting)

KRAMER. We have to bring this to an end now, but why don't you sum up at least, in a few sentences, the direction you feel Yiddish poetry has been moving in, since the Second World War. It's a big subject.

GREEN. Yes. Yes. One might say that the Holocaust left its very deep imprint on Jewish poets and Yiddish poetry throughout the world. It became one of the main subjects in Yiddish poetry for a number of years, and will still be, because many of us feel—as Leivick said—"Ich bin in Treblinka nit geven"—with a sense of guilt. We all feel *(weeping openly)* that we lived and—in a way—died together.

KRAMER. Part of us.

GREEN. Part of us . . . with the victims of Hitlerism. Because Hitlerism also destroyed physically many, many of our best poets—so, since then, our poets—Yiddish poets of any camp—became closer to the Yiddish people, closer to Jewish identity—

KRAMER. And the Yiddish word—

GREEN.—to the Yiddish word, to Yiddish life, the Yiddish language and literature, and they developed their talent; they became more serious; they came to acknowledge the importance of literature—that it has a peculiar function, a social function—

KRAMER. They had a greater integrity and commitment.

GREEN. Correct. Their feeling—their sense of commitment, grew. And as poets, practically each and every one writes with great commitment . . . when, for many years, they would think that poetry was just

248

a play, a thing of amusement—a thing to play around with words . . .
you don't find one now with such an approach.

KRAMER. It's a sacred mission. They know that now.

GREEN. Now they know that poetry has a great social and national
function, with obligations, duties, and responsibilities. And the same
trend takes place in Israel, in the Soviet Union now, among the poets
who survived . . . in Latin America especially . . . so that I personally
predict that our Yiddish poetry will have a great future, no doubt
about it.

June 28 (third meeting)

Under the mistaken belief that the end of the previous interview had
failed to be recorded, I tried to get Green to restate his summation.
This he did with admirable recall; in fact, he went beyond his first
statement.

GREEN. I also feel, and I can see it with my own eyes, that there is
a greater attachment between the Yiddish poets of today and the peo-
ple, the Jewish people—People with a capital P—as a whole—more
attachment to the history and literature of the Jewish people created
during centuries. I feel that they are going in the way of more *Yiddish-
kait,* not necessarily in a religious sense but in a broad historical and
national sense.

KRAMER. National, but not nationalist.

GREEN. Not nationalistic—a national sense. National in the sense
of being identified completely with the Jewish people—their suffer-
ings, their problems—

KRAMER.—and their hopes, their yearnings—

GREEN.—their reality, and their hopes for the future. So that I feel
very optimistic about it; I can see that during the last decades Yiddish
poetry as such has grown a great deal in content and in form, in vigor,
in self-expression, in searching for new and better methods—

KRAMER.—and the use of the word itself . . . the Yiddish word.

GREEN. Yes—and the use of the Yiddish word itself. They never
studied Yiddish as now. They never studied Jewish history, Jewish
holidays, events in the Jewish past, as now. So that I should end on a
note of hope and consolation to all those who suffered so much under
Hitlerism.

KRAMER. If we had had time last week, I would have followed your statement by saying—there are indeed figures in the Yiddish literary world who feel very differently than you do on this subject, and whose response would be perhaps the exact opposite of what yours is now. Maybe not in terms of style, but in terms of optimism.

GREEN. Well, as long as the Jewish people will exist, there will exist Yiddish poetry, Yiddish literature. As long as the last Jewish man will exist *(weeps openly)*, there will be Jewish poetry, because every human being, and of course every Jew, has a song in him, has poetry in him, whether or not it's expressed through words . . .

Aaron Kramer

A Tribute

MATTHEW PARIS

In America we like our poets to be like characters in newspapers or on television, yawping dionysically, or like monks adding a few lapidary words to dense verse like many-faceted coral. If they are not instantly sensational or mildly boring, we dismiss them as churls or leaden moralists and take up fare more palatable to the tastes of our age. If we are snobs, we vary this eternal exotic lunch with a few itinerant Brits of a wry familiarly monkish character that we sample on educational television.

Aaron Kramer did not have an English accent, was not addicted to anything, was married with children, and had no hunger for Scythian orgies run by Tibetan despots in exile in Colorado. He never evangelized for new gods or demanded world revolution. As a consequence, he lived a life that escaped all the clichés his country associated with rock stars and poets. Aaron married his childhood sweetheart, a girl who lived next door to him when he was nine years old, in Bath Beach, Brooklyn. His parents were Depression survivors; his mother is still living in California as I write this. She is ninety-nine years old.

He was a prodigy. His musical virtuosity with language was in place and intact when he was a young adolescent in high school. He went to Brooklyn College when he was barely sixteen; he was always younger than his colleagues and thus consistently in awe of them when he was a star in the college literary magazine.

Aaron was immediately recognized both at Brooklyn College and in fashionable leftist circles as a singular poet of talent, power, and intelligence. There was never any time in Aaron's life after thirteen when he was not mildly famous in a local way. We tend to assume these poets of social realism were Whitmanesque. Most poets like Aaron needed and valued a virtuosic formality of style to control material that was naturally open-ended and even obscure. Aaron and his peers modeled themselves after Auden, not Whitman. Auden was at Brooklyn College at the time. Auden offered them a poetic manner that mirrored their sense of their own natural aristocracy. Any one who

251

could write like Aaron had to be treated presumptively, if one viewed him through the mirrors of the Old World and its royalism, as like Auden, a kind of bastard lord.

Like most of his generation, he was schooled early in finding his subjects in newspapers. As late as the 1950s, Howard Fast rejected a large collection of Aaron's selected poems because it contained two small verses about his personal life. Fast considered this a sinister backsliding toward an affirmation of a nefarious individual reality. Aaron usually scorned wit as trivial, but this irate rejection and Fast's reasons amused him.

I don't know how much Aaron struggled for his virtues; he was a natural. It never struck him that one could or should be other than honest, brave, moral, generous, and charitable. He never looked into the abyss of his own evil; it wasn't there. Aaron took a clobbering from the communists because he was a maverick and, in his way, a serious Jew. He also was not all that popular among the anticommunist professors who were busy both betraying their colleagues and concocting a history of American poetry that did not include any realism or social criticism whatsoever.

Aaron took no sides; he loved diversity and excellence, not polemics. The original and new excited him. One of his favorite poets was Tennyson. The broadness of his appreciation of both life and art was phenomenal in a world that was largely polarized. When Aaron spoke up against tyranny in any form, it was like breathing. He didn't really get mad at anybody. He was a chamber mystic who loved freedom as a patriot of our species, not a lobotomized soldier. His impeccable fairness made all sides on any vulgar argument uncomfortable.

Aaron's virtue and honor were sterling almost to a fault; knowing him, one became aware that his was an instinctual perfection rather than an awkward Augustinian journey to goodness. It never occurred to him to do any evil or injury to anyone. His goodness seemed biological; he seemed to have a gene for virtue. Excess, experiments in moral relativism, any sort of cult or polemical stance simply could not appeal to Aaron. He brushed them away like flies. He didn't bother to reject such parochial notions; they were not worthy of notice to him.

Aaron once told me he had not published a very long satirical poem in imitation of Heine's travels because he thought it too savage in its denunciations. I always wanted to read this poem, but he never showed it to me. I couldn't imagine Aaron going after anything or anybody like Catullus or Juvenal. I wanted to see him try. He said he did it, and somewhere it lies, waiting for us, because Aaron thought—I could see it on his face—that savage indignation was unworthy of him.

His bravery was both consistent and casual; like the Chinese philosophers, Aaron wouldn't give evil the homage of a shrug. Aaron spoke of the Second World War primarily as a theater in which many people died, including his friends. He mourned not the destruction of states but the end of their personal hopes. Predictably he was very anti-McCarthy and equally anti-Red, for the same reasons: he was against anything that was reductive, that vulgarized diversity, that tried to put its stamp on the natural richness of the human spirit. For Aaron, this diversity in nature represented God's will on earth.

Aaron was a lyric poet who wrote in two phases: first, political, and second, personal. The bulk of his original work is a masterful set of verses extending from an idea with Euclidean linear force. In his youth his poems were socially minded; in his early middle age his poetry focused relentlessly on ordinary living much as did Montaigne's. There is a veiled rapture and despair in Aaron's work, but it is quiet, muted, measured. His verse is never gaudy or sensational, never strains to shock or to produce some spectacular effect. Aaron would have thought such aims uncivil. Perhaps they are.

Aaron was one of the greatest masters of rhyme and meter in English. He could do anything. Like Tennyson, he was a great master of rhyme and assonance. Unlike Tennyson, his lines are never suffused with erotic hungers or heroic tragedy. Aaron never took up an impolite emotion. His Augustan character took him to modes of a high consciousness and meditation rather than celebrations of puerile erotic lust or heroic warlike epics. Although they did not resemble each other in any superficial way, one might think of Aaron as an American Gerard Manley Hopkins. Both men testified in idiosyncratic verse to the light and dark of personal mortality.

Obviously a man like this in a country like this was very likely to fall through the cracks. Aaron only half fell. Poets reading Aaron may or may not feel cheated by the lack of shallow and rampant erotica and the rude dearth of violence in his verse. But if they have craft, they have to be stunned by Aaron's sheer poetic gift. Aaron was that good a pure poet.

Aaron wondered whether he should have taken up excess or risked something large at some point in his life so he could be the sort of intrepid poet who was always in recovery from major neural trauma. Aaron didn't miss that some poets, like Shakespeare, left the world verse that recorded terrible primal suffering. Of course, many men have lived lives of torture and have never written even a limerick that might amuse the future. Aaron never repaired to the universal hospital where many poets take up residence in retrospective romance, despair, and subsequent hyperbole. "I'm too good at too many small things," Aaron said to me a few times. It wasn't that. Aaron was a natural man of virtue living in an age whose concern was vice.

Aaron suspected that he had everything to be a great poet but the proper major disaster. Yet Aaron was drawn to such poets in his translations. Heine, after all, is a rather intense and passionate personality. Aaron could take up these themes at a distance. But his life of writing and teaching, first in the New York public high schools, then at Dowling College in Long Island, was generously and successfully happy and measured. Poets don't thrive in a world that is fascinated by bad guys if they have the misfortune to be good guys.

Aaron was a serious Jew without being metaphysically religious. He easily took up the high ethical character of his traditions. Teaching was a moral and spiritual act for him, not a job. He never could stop doing it. I think Aaron would have been at home in eighteenth-century England or America. That was the last time in Western history people valued measure and reason. As a man and a poet, he seems to have been born in the wrong time. The age that valued Pope would have appreciated him. When the future learns respect for virtue again, it will turn to Aaron.

Aaron Kramer first gained national prominence with *Seven Poets in Search of an Answer* (1944) and *The Poetry and Prose of Heinrich Heine* (1948). He was a leading resistance poet throughout the McCarthy era, with such texts for music as *Denmark Vesey* and such volumes as *Roll the Forbidden Drums!* In 1958, he collaborated with a dozen artists on *The Tune of Calliope: Poems and Drawings of New York*. Professor of English at Dowling College since 1961, and founding coeditor of *West Hills Review: A Whitman Journal*, he produced such scholarly works as *The Prophetic Tradition in American Poetry* (1968), and *Melville's Poetry: Toward the Enlarged Heart* (1972). The same year, he edited the Macmillan anthology *On Freedom's Side: American Poets of Protest*.

Equally noted as a translator, Kramer produced *Rilke: Visions of Christ* in 1967 and an English version of *The Emperor of Atlantis* in 1975; this work, created in the death camp of Terezin, was premiered by the San Francisco Opera in 1977 and has subsequently been performed in many countries, most recently at Philadelphia's Curtis Institute. In 1989, 370 of Dr. Kramer's translations from the work of 135 Yiddish poets appeared in a widely praised anthology, *A Century of Yiddish Poetry*, which he also edited. The most recent collections of his own poems are *Carousel Parkway* (1980), two 1983 volumes, *The Burning Bush* and *In Wicked Times*, and *Indigo and Other Poems* (1991). He also had a chapter in *Life Guidance Through Literature*, 1992, and authored numerous articles on poetry for the disabled, a field in which he pioneered. *Oblomov*, a musical play for which he provided the lyrics, was recently showcased at New York's Cubicolo Theatre by the National Shakespeare Company.

Dr. Kramer was a popular public reader on both coasts for decades; over eighty of his radio broadcasts are archived, and he recorded for Folkways Records as well as for the Library of Congress. In 1993, he received a National Endowment for the Humanities grant. His work as translator was honored with a festschrift volume: *The Second First*

Art: Poetry in Translation and Essays on the Art of Translating. In 1995, Kramer translated a bilingual collection of poems by Dora Teitelboim entitled *All My Yesterdays Were Steps.* Dr. Kramer received his Ph.D. at New York University.

Saul Lishinsky was born in Carbondale, Illinois, and lived most of his life in New York City. He earned his degree from New York City University. Lishinsky has exhibited his works extensively both at home and abroad, including solo shows in Lisbon, Denver, and Connecticut and group shows in New York City, Denver, and New Jersey. In addition, he published his drawings and poems in 1958 in a collection entitled *The Tune of the Calliope: Poems and Drawings of New York,* in 1973 in *Soundview Throgs Neck Community Mental Health Center Newsletter,* and in 1980 in *Art Therapy Viewpoints.* Lishinsky is proud of his work in art therapy; he has published articles in this area and instructed professional artists and amateurs in the psychiatric treatment of patients through art therapy.

Lishinsky has been an active muralist, unveiling his skills in 1977 and 1979 at the Westchester Square branch of the New York Public Library in works titled *Celebration I* and *Celebration II,* respectively. In 1978, he exhibited *New York, New York* at Julia Richmond High School and in 1982, *Castle Hill Youth Murals* at Castle Hill Community Center. He has also displayed numerous murals in Manhattan and in the Bronx. He is a member of Young American Artists, Creative Artists Association, Westbeth Residents Council, Westbeth Studio Arts Group, and American Art Therapy Association.

About this book, Lishinsky remarks:

> These are not illustrations in the usual sense; their images often do not match those in the poems they face. Instead, an attempt is made to reflect and probe the poems' meaning, the expression of changing life from which the poem comes.
>
> In the drawings and paintings in this book, I meditate on our contemporary "Inferno." With these images, I aspire to achieve the haunting quality that comes from deepened layers of meaning, rendered in whatever variation of style is chosen. If the viewer and reader of this book is thereby engaged in a parallel meditation, I will have achieved my purpose.